ISBN:979-8-9990779-3-6

This book is intended as a practical resource and informational guide. It is not a substitute for professional counseling or therapy. The author and publisher assume no liability for outcomes related to the use of this book.

# The Monk at Gate B12

Mastering Life With Stillness, Discipline, and Strategy

by

Ethan Starke

4

This book was not written to impress.
It was written to endure.

To honor stillness.
To protect discipline.
To guide through strategy.

6

For my teachers,
the seen and the unseen.

*"Only when you can be extremely pliable and soft can you be extremely hard and strong."*
— Zen Proverb

# Preface:

# The Monk at Gate B12

---

October 2015.
Frankfurt Airport. Gate B12.

I had just finished my first international event as a "futurist."
Recognition I wasn't sure I deserved, applause I hadn't yet
learned to trust.
It opened the door to a life I thought I wanted — the kind of life
that looks good in headlines and sounds impressive in airport
lounges.

A "futurist" with no plans for his future.
That was me that day.
Wisdom was not what I was keen to have before heading to my
gate — but coffee, yes.
I was going home, back to a life that was about to shift from first
into fourth gear, and a career I never planned was about to lift me
off the ground — and keep me there, airborne, for the next four
years.

Between 2015 and 2019, I would live out of a suitcase, chasing
opportunities across the world.
In 2018 alone, Google tracked my movements: I traveled the
equivalent of six and a half times around the Earth.

On the surface, it looked like success.
Underneath, it was something else — speed without direction, achievement without anchoring.

But I didn't know that yet.

That afternoon, I sat waiting for my flight when he took the seat across from me.
A head-shaved man, my height but sturdy like an oak tree.
A worn bag.
The kind of presence you notice without trying.
My age, maybe a few years older — calm, centered, and in no way there to please.
As if the space around him operated by different rules.

I don't remember how the conversation started.
Something about the weather, maybe, or the way airports blur all sense of time.

He didn't ask what I did.
He wasn't interested in small talk.

Instead, he asked me a question:

> *"How do you chop a tree 1,000 kilometers away?"*

I gave the kind of answer you give when you're tired and trying to be polite.
*"I'm against chopping trees,"* I said.

He smiled — and said nothing.

As his flight was called and he stood to leave, he paused, looking at me as if seeing something I didn't know was visible.

> *"You already know,"* he said. *"But you are not yet seeing."*

And then he was gone.

I didn't know who he was.
I didn't know what he meant.
I didn't know that I would reach the highest pinnacle of a career
in the next few years — only to watch everything I thought I had
built collapse.
Material, self-worth, identity, and purpose — all the things I had
spent years curating — would vanish.

I didn't know that his words — strange, vague, forgettable —
would come back to me.
Not once. Not twice. But over and over.
Like a riddle I couldn't solve.
Like a lighthouse I didn't know I would need.

This book is not about riddles.
And it's not about what I lost — or even what I found.

It's about how to crack the code and live above the noise.
It's about what I learned to see.

---

# Chapter 1

# The Life I Thought I Had

Success is a strange thing when it comes fast.
You don't question it — you sprint to keep up with it.
You don't examine it — you perform it.

After that event in Frankfurt, everything accelerated.
Projects piled up. Clients found me faster than I could handle.
Speaking invitations, partnerships, new ventures — doors that
had always been locked seemed to swing open on their own.
I said yes to almost everything.

Why wouldn't I?
When you've spent years unseen, you don't decline the spotlight
when it finally turns your way.
You step in. You run faster. You work harder. You prove you
deserve it — not just to others, but to yourself.

For a while, it even felt like freedom.
No office. No routine. No borders.
The life I was building was mobile, borderless, liquid.
I lived in hotel rooms, worked from airport lounges, took
meetings across time zones without ever really landing anywhere.

In 2018 alone, my passport accumulated more stamps than most people see in a lifetime.
Google Maps told me I had traveled the distance of six and a half times around the globe.
I lived out of a suitcase. I memorized flight numbers. I knew the difference between a good and bad airport coffee by the smell alone.

On paper, it looked perfect.
In conversation, it sounded impressive.
Online, it was easy to package and display.

But reality is quieter than presentation.
Success is louder than self-awareness.

---

I told myself I was building something.
A career. A reputation. A future.

But when the rush wears off — and it always does — what's left is not the applause, not the milestones, not the photos.
What's left is the rhythm of your life.
The part no one else sees.
The part you can't edit or perform.

And my rhythm was chaos — polished chaos, curated chaos, but chaos all the same.
No real plans. No real home.
No long view.
Just the next opportunity, and the one after that.

What I didn't understand then is something I see now:
**Speed can make you feel powerful, but only stillness can make you clear.**

I wasn't building a future.

I was chasing an illusion — one success at a time, faster, faster, faster — hoping the next achievement would finally feel like arrival.

It never did.

---

At the time, though, it was easy to ignore the quiet signals.

You tell yourself tiredness is a badge of honor.
You treat burnout like an upgrade.
You believe motion is the same as direction.

It's easy to confuse the two when everyone around you is doing the same.
The problem isn't just that you can't see clearly — it's that you don't even realize you're blind.

I didn't see it then.
But looking back, I can trace it easily.

The signs were there, faint but persistent:

- The uneasy sense that achievements were coming faster than meaning.

- The creeping feeling that if I stopped moving, everything would collapse.

- The hollow victories that lasted a moment, maybe two, before dissolving into the need for the next.

---

It showed up in small ways at first.
In the details I used to notice but no longer did.

Like the time I woke up in a hotel in Singapore and forgot what city I was in.
Not for a second — but for a minute that stretched longer than it should have.
I remember sitting on the edge of the bed, scanning the curtains, the carpet, the view — looking for a clue.
When the answer finally clicked — Marina Bay Sands, the skyline, the smell of the room — I laughed it off.
*Too many flights*, I told myself. *Just tired.*

Or the time I agreed to a meeting in London without realizing it overlapped with another in New York — until two assistants emailed me reminders within minutes of each other.
I didn't cancel either.
I split my time, appeared in one by video from the backseat of a cab, the other half an hour late, bleary-eyed and smiling as if the delay were just traffic.

Everyone laughed.
No one noticed.
But I noticed.

---

I noticed it most in the quiet spaces — the moments between flights, between meetings, between applause.
The moments when the noise faded just enough for the silence to creep in.
It was in those gaps that I would sometimes remember the monk.
Not his face, not the details — just the feeling of him.
The way the space around him felt slower, heavier, more anchored.

And sometimes, if I was tired enough or still enough, I could almost hear his voice again:

*"You already know. But you are not yet seeing."*

It would pass, of course.
I would take another call, answer another email, book another flight.
The riddle would recede into the background.
And I would return to the chase.

---

That was the life I thought I had built.
Fast. Impressive. Unsustainable.
A structure with no foundation — weightless, but somehow heavy.

I would live like that for a few more years.
Long enough to forget the monk's words.
Long enough to believe, for a while, that I had outrun the riddle he had left me with.

---

## The Question I Couldn't Answer

---

Grief has no edges.
You don't know where it begins or ends — only that you're inside it.

When my father passed away in 2017, I did what people like me are trained to do:
I kept moving.

Work became the cure.
Travel became the therapy.
I filled every blank space with momentum, every silence with departure boards and hotel check-ins.
As if movement could undo loss.
As if motion could erase the weight.

---

Somewhere in the middle of it all, my body began to protest.
A torn rotator cuff from handling luggage — more flights than I could count, more bags than I could carry.
The kind of injury that demands rest.
The kind of injury I didn't have time to acknowledge.

I worked through it.
I smiled through it.
I wore pain like an accessory — invisible but ever-present.
If I kept going, maybe it would go away.
If I kept going, maybe I wouldn't have to notice what was underneath it.

---

The collapse didn't happen all at once.
It came in layers, quiet at first.

My business partner walked out — no warning, no ceremony.
One minute we were building something, the next it was rubble.
The business I thought was permanent revealed itself to be a

house of cards — and with it, the version of myself that was attached to it began to unravel too.

Still, I moved.
Still, I worked.
Still, I told myself this was a phase, a recalibration, not an ending.

---

Then came Beirut.
The collapse of the banking sector was not a correction — it was an erasure.
Currency devalued — five million dollars, gone.
Penniless in a country where even survival had become a negotiation.

I didn't even have the luxury of mourning it.
There were bigger losses.

---

August 2020.
A man-made disaster tore through Beirut — one of the largest non-nuclear explosions in history.
I survived.
The word sounds victorious.
It isn't.

Survival is not a victory when the blast leaves holes in the city and deeper ones inside you.
Survival is an echo.
It's silence where there should be sound.
It's knowing you are alive, but not being sure why.

---

Loss doesn't care about sequencing.
It doesn't space itself out politely.

Before I could steady myself, I lost my nephew — fifteen years old.
A kind of loss that has no shape, no narrative, no explanation.
A hole that doesn't heal.

---

By 2021, the ground beneath me had disappeared completely.
I relocated to Houston with what was left of my life.
No safety net.
No plan.
No home.

There's a line between struggling and sinking.
I crossed it quietly.

I don't talk much about what those days felt like.
There are things language can't hold.
But I know what the edge of despair looks like.
I know how convincing it can be.
I know what it means to consider vanishing.
And I know what it means for someone to pull you back.

It wasn't a grand intervention.
It wasn't a dramatic rescue.
It was a phone call from my Rabbi — one human voice refusing to let me disappear.
Sometimes survival is not a choice you make.
It's a choice someone makes for you.

---

After that, silence.
Not peace — silence.

No job to run to.
No meetings to take.
No applause to chase.

Just silence.
And in that silence, the monk returned.

---

I don't mean I saw him.
I don't mean I heard his voice.

I mean his words resurfaced — words I had filed away under interesting, forgotten, irrelevant:

*"You already know. But you are not yet seeing."*

At first, they felt like a taunt.
A reminder of how much I had lost, how little I had understood.
But the more I sat with them — not fought them, not analyzed them — the more they began to sound different.

Not a rebuke.
Not a judgment.
A map.
A map I hadn't been ready for.
A map I had needed all along.

---

Grief has no edges.
But sometimes, if you stay still long enough, you can find the shape beneath it.
The pattern.

The current.
The invisible structure under the noise.

The monk wasn't offering me an answer.
He was offering me a way to see.

But first, I had to learn how to look.

---

## Searching for the Lighthouse

---

When you lose everything, the world doesn't stop spinning.
It just stops spinning for you.

The lights stay on.
The flights keep taking off.
People keep moving, laughing, living — as if gravity works
differently for them.

When I landed in Houston, I was carrying more than a duffle bag.
I was carrying a life I didn't recognize anymore.
Loss has a way of stripping you — not just of money, or plans, or
titles — but of identity.
You don't just lose things; you lose the person you thought you
were.

---

In the beginning, I did what I had always done:
I tried to outrun the silence.

I looked for work.
I made plans.

But the old moves didn't work anymore.
The old strategies, the ones that once opened doors, now led to empty rooms.
The network I had built — flights, meetings, deals — felt thin, distant, like a currency no one was accepting anymore.

There's a point where effort becomes noise.
And when the noise gets loud enough, you have to choose:
Keep fighting it, or sit still and listen to what's underneath it.

For the first time in years, I sat still.
Not because I wanted to.
Because I didn't have the strength to do anything else.

And in that stillness, something unexpected happened:
I started to feel the edges of things again.
Not clear, not sharp — just the faint outlines of questions I had been too busy to ask.

---

The monk's words kept resurfacing.
Not aggressively.
Like a ripple under the surface of water.

> *"You already know. But you are not yet seeing."*

At first, they made me angry.
What did I know?
If I knew something, why had I lost everything?
If I could see, why hadn't I seen it coming?

But anger fades faster than questions do.
And once the anger drained out, the question remained:
What was I not seeing?

---

I didn't set out on a spiritual journey.
I didn't buy a one-way ticket to India.
I didn't meditate under a tree or attend a silent retreat.

I started smaller.
Quieter.

I reread old notes.
Listened to conversations I had recorded but never really heard.
Went back to the few fragments of the monk's conversation I could remember, turning them over like stones in my hand.

And slowly — very slowly — I started to notice a pattern.

Not an answer.
Not yet.
Just a pattern.

---

When I looked back at the people I had admired — the ones who had built lives, not just careers — I saw something I hadn't noticed before.

They moved slower.
They saw deeper.
They didn't chase every opportunity — they waited for the ones that fit.
They didn't react — they *observed, anticipated, acted only when necessary.*

Their lives weren't built on noise.
They were built on something quieter, something sturdier.

It wasn't speed that made them successful.
It was something else.

Stillness.
Discipline.
Strategy.

---

I didn't have words for it yet.
I didn't have a framework.
All I had was the sense that there was a lighthouse somewhere out there — not a destination, not a rescue, but a direction.
Something solid to steer toward, even if I couldn't see it clearly yet.

I started reading again — but not the books I used to read.
Not productivity hacks.
Not business manuals.
I found myself pulled toward older ideas — traditions built on endurance, on patience, on unseen work.
Zen teachings.
Stoic philosophy.
And eventually — inevitably — Shaolin.

---

The more I read, the more the shape of the thing I was looking for began to form.
Shaolin wasn't just martial arts.
It wasn't about fighting at all.

It was about seeing.

Waiting.

Training beyond exhaustion — not to win faster, but to endure longer.

Not to defeat others, but to master yourself.

It wasn't new.

It was ancient.

Older than every system I had built my previous life around.

Older than the noise.

---

Stillness.

Discipline.

Strategy.

These weren't tactics.

They were fluencies — learned slowly, patiently, invisibly.

The monk hadn't given me a secret.

He had given me a riddle — one I could only answer by changing how I moved through the world.

But first, I would have to learn to see the patterns.

The ones that had been there all along.

---

# The Underground Work

*Before he was allowed to touch a staff, the young monk spent seven years sweeping the monastery grounds.*

*No lessons, no sparring, no shortcuts — only the rhythm of the broom, day after day.*

*When he asked when his training would begin, his master said only:*
*"It already has."*

*His name was Liu Jinbao — who later became one of the grandmasters who revived Shaolin teachings in the modern era.*

*She scribbled in the margins of napkins, in cafes and buses, pushing a stroller with one hand, writing with the other.*
*Twelve publishers rejected her manuscript.*

*It would take seven years, a dozen rejections, and a thousand unseen hours before the world saw what she saw.*

*Her name was J.K. Rowling.*

*He worked at a patent office, filing other people's ideas.*
*No lab, no academic post, no research grants.*
*Just a desk and equations scribbled on scraps of paper in his free hours.*

*It was there that he first outlined the theory of relativity.*

*His name was Albert Einstein.*

*He missed 5,000 shots.*
*Lost 300 games.*
*Failed 26 times to make the winning shot — and kept*
*shooting.*

*Failure wasn't the end.*
*It was the practice.*

*His name was Michael Jordan.*

*After closing his jazz bar at midnight, he sat at a
small table and wrote by hand.
No agent, no publisher, no fans — just words on a
page in the quiet hours when no one else was
watching.*


*Years later, he became one of the most translated
novelists in the world..*


*His name was Haruki Murakami.*

*In high school, after regular practice ended, he stayed in the gym and shot 1,000 baskets alone in the dark.*
*No crowd.*
*No cameras.*
*No guarantee.*

*Shot by shot, hour by hour, he built what talent alone never could.*

*His name was Kobe Bryant.*

*A boy sat still for hours, legs aching, back straight,*
*facing a blank wall.*
*No fighting.*
*No glory.*
*No promises.*


*When he finally moved, he didn't think about timing.*
*He was timing.*


*His name was Shi Yan Ming.*

*The world loves overnight success stories.*
*But the truth lives underground — where no one is*
*looking.*


*Mastery isn't a flash.*
*It's a slow burn.*


*This is not about hacks.*
*This is about fluency — built in silence, discipline,*
*and time.*

---

# Chapter 2

# The Past Is Always Prologue

## Why the Future Is Predictable — to Those Who Study the Past

If you listen closely, the future doesn't sound like chaos.
It sounds like an echo.

Most people believe the future is uncertain — unknowable,
unpredictable, random.
But the ones who survive — and more often, the ones who thrive
— know better.
The future is rarely new.
It is almost always a variation of something old.

Technology changes. Styles shift. Markets rise and fall.
But beneath the surface, human behavior hums the same familiar
song it has sung for centuries.
We respond to fear and greed the way we always have.
We build and destroy and rebuild along the same invisible lines.
We fall in love, fall apart, rise, collapse, retreat, and advance in
rhythms that outlast dynasties and trends.

The future does not require prophecy to understand.
It requires memory.
It requires pattern recognition.

History, properly read, is not a museum.
It is a mirror.

The same drives that shaped the ancient world shape the modern one — only the costumes have changed.
We are not inventing new emotions, new follies, new ambitions.
We are rehearsing old ones under different lights.

To the untrained eye, the future looks chaotic.
To those who study the past, it looks predictable — not in its details, but in its movements.
They don't guess what will happen next; they recognize the cadence of what always happens.

History never repeats itself exactly, but it rhymes.
And for those who can hear it, the rhyme is unmistakable.

---

## Repeating Cycles in History, Markets, and Human Behavior

---

The world does not move in straight lines.
It circles.
It spirals.
It repeats itself with slight variations, like a melody played in different keys across different generations.

The more closely you study the past, the more you notice the repetition — not exact, but faithful enough to predict the next movement if you are willing to look beyond the surface.

Empires do not fall suddenly; they follow a rhythm.
First comes the rise — built on discipline, innovation, unity.
Then the flourish — wealth, expansion, triumph.
Inevitably, decadence follows: disconnection from original values, indulgence, internal decay.
By the time collapse arrives, it feels sudden to the unprepared, but to those who know the pattern, it was written long before the walls crumbled.

Rome did not fall in a day.
Neither did the British Empire, nor any civilization that mistook its height for permanence.
Cycles of power are not accidents; they are inheritances of human nature — pride, overreach, neglect.

Markets behave no differently.
Every bubble begins in optimism, expands into mania, and collapses under the weight of its own excess.
From the tulip mania in 17th century Holland to the speculative fevers of the 1920s, to the housing collapse of 2008 and beyond — the story does not change.
Only the assets do.

Greed has a pattern.
Fear has a pattern.
They alternate like seasons.

Even in our private lives, the same cycles replay.
Relationships spark with excitement, settle into routine, and fray under the quiet erosion of neglect.

Careers ascend on ambition, plateau in comfort, and decline when curiosity and effort are replaced by entitlement.

Growth is cyclical.
Decline is cyclical.
Reinvention, too, follows its rhythm.

And yet, most live in denial of this.
We convince ourselves that *this time* is different.
We believe we have transcended history, outsmarted the cycle.
We behave as though success will extend indefinitely, as if decline is for others, as if collapse cannot touch us.

But the cycle does not spare the unaware.
It humbles the proud and rewards the prepared.

To understand history is not to memorize dates or revere old victories.
It is to study the motion beneath the motion — the slow tides that lift and lower civilizations, markets, and individual lives alike.

To see these patterns is to understand that while you cannot control the cycle, you can learn to move with it.
You can plant in spring, harvest in summer, store in fall, and endure the winter without panic.
You can refuse to mistake the moment for forever.

Cycles do not promise safety.
But they do offer predictability — for those who have the patience to see them and the discipline to act accordingly.

# The Illusion of Newness — Why Most Trends Are Echoes

We like to believe we live in unprecedented times.
The world markets itself as new, and we — wanting to be original, exceptional — are eager to believe it.

We celebrate innovation, invention, disruption, as if these are forces never before seen.
Each generation declares its uniqueness, its break from the past.
Each one is wrong.

What we call newness is usually repetition in finer clothes.

The "sharing economy" of the early twenty-first century — hailed as a technological revolution — was little more than an ancient barter system draped in apps and algorithms.
Long before ride shares and home rentals had venture capital valuations, communities exchanged labor and shelter without middlemen.

Cryptocurrency, for all its futuristic vocabulary, echoed humanity's oldest instinct: to build a currency of trust when institutions lose credibility.
Gold, silver, shells, paper, now digital coins — different forms, same need.

Cancel culture, too, is no modern phenomenon.
Public shaming has ancient roots — the stocks and pillories of

41

medieval towns, the excommunications of religious institutions, the banishments of courts and kings.
The methods have changed.
The impulse remains.

Even fashion, the most visible theater of novelty, moves not forward but in circles.
Hemlines rise and fall predictably.
Minimalism returns after indulgence, only to give way again to extravagance.
The colors, the cuts, the fabrics vary, but the rhythms do not.

Technology seduces us with its apparent acceleration, but the patterns underneath remain unbroken.
The printing press was once condemned for undermining religious authority, just as the internet was feared for undermining the gatekeepers of information.
New machines, old anxieties.

We confuse new tools with new behaviors, forgetting that fear, greed, pride, and ambition are constants.
The shape of our tools evolves, but the hands that wield them do not.

Every so-called revolution — social, technological, cultural — is less an explosion of novelty and more a reshuffling of ancient instincts.
We dress old desires in new language and call it progress.

This is not cynicism.
It is clarity.

To see through the illusion of newness is not to dismiss change, but to understand its limits.

The surface may glitter, but the currents underneath are slow, deep, and familiar.

The wise do not mistake the wave for the tide.

They recognize that what dazzles others as disruption is often little more than an echo — louder, perhaps, but still only an echo — of what has always been.

---

# Lessons from History's Ignored Patterns

---

Patterns, once ignored, do not fade quietly into the background.
They wait — patient, silent — until their neglect demands a price.

History is littered with the wreckage of those who thought they could outrun the cycle.
Collapse never comes without warning.
It only comes without being believed.

Rome did not fall because it was attacked.
It fell because, long before the Visigoths breached its walls, the empire had already hollowed itself out from within.
Discipline decayed into decadence.
Civic duty gave way to personal ambition.
Citizens became spectators, content to trade freedom for entertainment, responsibility for spectacle.

The signs were there — widening inequality, crumbling infrastructure, fractured politics — but it is the nature of decline to be ignored by those most invested in the illusion of permanence.

So Rome did not fall.
It rotted.
And when it finally collapsed, the surprise belonged only to the willfully blind.

The 2008 financial crisis offers no less a lesson.
The collapse of markets was not a mystery; it was a consequence.
Warnings had echoed through the system — analysts, economists, cautious voices whispering about unsustainable debt, reckless speculation, houses bought with money no one really had.
But in times of prosperity, warnings sound like pessimism.
And no one likes a pessimist when the sun is shining.

What could have been corrected early was denied late.
And so the correction came, brutally, inevitably.

Even disasters born from human error follow these patterns.
Chernobyl was not a surprise; it was the last domino in a line that had been falling quietly for years.
Ignored warnings.
Underestimated risks.
A system designed to conceal rather than confront failure.

Each time, the disaster felt sudden only because the signs were ignored for so long.

But it is not only nations and industries that suffer from the refusal to recognize patterns.
Individuals suffer, too.

The marriage that ends with slammed doors and silence usually began its decline years earlier — with a thousand small neglects, with conversations left unspoken, grievances left unhealed.

44

The career that collapses under the weight of burnout did not fall overnight; it cracked slowly, as purpose was traded for promotions, meaning sacrificed for motion.

Patterns are patient.
They do not force recognition.
They wait — until the cost of ignorance is unavoidable.

The true tragedy is not that collapse happens.
Collapse is natural.
Cycles rise and fall.
The tragedy is that most collapses are not random acts of fate.
They are failures of attention.

We are given signals — in history, in markets, in relationships, in our own bodies and minds —
but we are trained to look away, to believe that what has come before will not come again,
that this time is different, that somehow we will be spared.

But the cycle does not spare the careless.
It humbles them.
It teaches — harshly — what it first tried to teach gently.

The price of ignoring patterns is paid not just in dollars or dynasties, but in years wasted, trust broken, lives derailed.

Patterns do not punish.
They simply proceed.

To ignore them is not brave.
It is blind.

And blindness, in a world of repeating rhythms, is not an accident.
It is a choice.

# How to Read Time Forward by Reading It Backward

Most people look forward and see only fog.
They squint into the distance, hoping to glimpse some shape of what's to come,
but the future does not reveal itself to those who stare into the unknown.
It reveals itself to those who study what has already been.

The future is not a mystery for those who know where to look.
It is a mirror, held just slightly askew.
It does not demand prophecy.
It demands memory.

Those who move with quiet confidence into the future are not guessing.
They are remembering.
They are reading the shape of things past and recognizing their faint outlines ahead.

The best strategists, investors, leaders, even the wisest individuals, do not make decisions by peering forward into chaos.
They look backward — not to relive old glories or regrets, but to find the rhythm hidden behind the noise.

The past is a map, imperfect but essential.
It shows not precise routes, but contours.
It reveals the mountains that are slow to rise and slow to fall, the

rivers that cut across generations, the fault lines that crack in every era though they shift position and name.

The further back you look, the further ahead you can see. Because while circumstances change, the architecture of human behavior does not.

The empires that crumbled under the weight of their own pride; the markets that collapsed under waves of unchecked greed; the relationships that withered from neglect rather than violence —

each of these leaves a shape in the soil.

The wise do not try to predict exact outcomes.
They read the currents.
They sense when the tide is turning, even when the water still seems calm.

They study history not for dates and events, but for patterns of rise and fall,
of boom and bust, of flourishing and fading.

They study their own histories, too.
They notice the subtle echoes that repeat in their choices —
the career moves that led to growth, the decisions that ended in regret,
the habits that built strength and the ones that slowly eroded it.

They learn to recognize the quiet signs that most ignore:
the tightening of fear before markets crack,
the overconfidence before innovation collapses under its own hype,
the small betrayals of routine before a relationship silently fractures.

Reading backward is not nostalgia.
It is reconnaissance.

It is preparing not by trying to guess what will come next,
but by understanding that what comes next is already whispering
—

not ahead of you, but behind you.

The past, if read carefully, reveals the future in outline.

It does not promise certainty.
But it promises clarity.

And clarity, in a world addicted to speed and noise,
is power.

The person who reads the past wisely does not panic when the
winds shift.
They do not chase the noise of each new trend.
They are not easily surprised, not easily rattled, not easily broken.

They move with a calm the world mistakes for luck.
It is not luck.
It is pattern recognition practiced patiently over time.

The past is a trail.
It is not behind you.
It is under your feet.
And it stretches forward further than you think.

---

# Chapter 3

# Training Your Pattern Eye

## Pattern Blindness — Why Most People Only See Noise

Most people live surrounded by patterns and never see them.
Not because the patterns are hidden,
but because their eyes are tuned to the wrong frequency.

We are born with a bias toward the immediate, the obvious, the loud.
The mind, left to its instincts, notices what moves quickly, what flashes, what demands attention.
It is not designed for subtlety.
It is designed for survival — to spot the predator in the grass, the lightning in the sky.

But what kept early humans alive in a hostile world is not what helps a modern mind navigate a complex one.
Speed and noise grab our attention.
Stillness and pattern escape it.

This blindness is not a defect.
It is the default setting.

The surface of life is full of noise — headlines, trends, crises, fads, panics.
Most people skim this surface endlessly, chasing the latest information without seeing the structure underneath it.
They believe they are informed because they consume more.
They believe they are prepared because they react faster.
But reaction is not perception.
And consumption is not understanding.

Noise overwhelms the senses.
It fills the mind with distractions, with fragments of information unconnected to anything deeper.
In this noise, patterns are drowned out like a melody smothered by static.

It is not that the patterns do not exist.
It is that most people never slow down enough to hear them.
They move too quickly, look too narrowly, live too reactively.

In a world addicted to immediacy, pattern blindness is epidemic.

We see the latest viral outrage but miss the cycle of public anger and amnesia it fits into.
We see the stock market rise or fall and react to the day's news without noticing the longer waves underneath.
We see the collapse of a relationship, a company, a country, and treat it as an isolated event —
forgetting how familiar the steps were that led there.

Noise is not just loud.
It is seductive.
It convinces you that knowing more is the same as knowing

better.
It trains you to value speed over depth, novelty over truth,
quantity over pattern.

But noise never teaches.
It only exhausts.

And exhaustion blinds you further —
until you are living on the surface of things, reacting to shadows,
mistaking activity for insight.

Pattern blindness is not an absence of intelligence.
It is an absence of stillness.
It is the inability to move slowly enough, patiently enough,
quietly enough, to notice what does not scream for attention.

It is not that most people are incapable of seeing patterns.
It is that they are too distracted to remember how.

---

## Cultivating Second-Order Observation

---

The first thing most people notice is what is in front of them.
The first-order facts — the event, the outcome, the surface.

But the surface is never the whole story.
And first-order observation, though easy, is rarely useful.

To see what others miss, you have to train yourself to look
beyond the first glance —
to trace not what is happening, but why it is happening,

not the immediate effect, but the deeper cause,
not the noise, but the current moving beneath it.

This is second-order observation.
It is not a gift.
It is a discipline.

It requires patience, because second-order signals are never loud.
They do not announce themselves.
They are subtle, quiet, often uncomfortable to face.
While the world chases the obvious, second-order observers
linger in the background, studying the terrain everyone else runs
past.

They look at what others overlook —
the small shifts before the earthquake,
the faint cracks before the collapse,
the slight tensions in a conversation before a relationship
fractures.

They resist the urge to react quickly.
They let events unfold long enough to reveal their patterns.
While others demand immediate clarity, second-order observers
are willing to live in the fog a little longer,
trusting that clarity, like patterns, reveals itself slowly to those
who are patient enough to wait.

Most people see the rise in markets and celebrate.
The second-order observer notices not just the rise, but the speed,
the leverage, the unsustainable optimism underneath.
They understand that what rises too fast is vulnerable to the fall.

Most people see a booming business and admire its growth.
The second-order observer studies its foundation —
Is the growth disciplined?

Are the customers loyal or simply chasing the latest trend?
Is the culture built to survive difficulty, or only expansion?

Most people see a scandal and react to the outrage.
The second-order observer studies what the scandal reveals —
the cracks in the system that made it inevitable.

This way of seeing is not about cynicism.
It is about depth.
It is about refusing to be fooled by appearances, however
convincing they may seem.

Second-order observation demands distance — not physical, but
emotional.
You must be willing to step back from your own hopes, fears,
biases.
You must observe not only the world but your own mind
observing it.
You must see not only the event, but the conditions that allowed
the event.

It is not easy.
It is not fast.
But it is powerful.

Second-order observers are not fortune-tellers.
They are mapmakers.
They see where the land rises and falls long before others notice
the slope.

And in a world that moves too fast for reflection,
the ability to see beyond the first-order appearance is not just rare.
It is an advantage.

# How to Sharpen Your Signal-to-Noise Ratio

The world offers more information today than at any point in human history.
Every day, the flood intensifies — news, commentary, opinion, speculation, distraction.
A constant current, pulling at your attention, demanding your reaction.

But more information does not mean more understanding.
In fact, it often leads to less.

The mind, like any instrument, has limits.
When it is overloaded, it loses the ability to distinguish what matters from what does not.
It confuses volume with value, movement with meaning.

Noise overwhelms signal.
The important drowns in the urgent.
The patterns are lost beneath the static.

The ability to sharpen your signal-to-noise ratio is the difference between clarity and confusion.
It is not about blocking information, but about filtering it — learning to hear the quiet rhythm beneath the chaos.

Sharpening this ability begins not with adding more, but with subtracting.
Subtraction is a discipline.

It demands that you step back from the flood and ask:
What is essential here?
What is real?
What repeats?
What endures?

Noise demands your immediate reaction —
another headline, another update, another surge of outrage or
enthusiasm.
Signal waits patiently to be found.
It does not shout.
It does not insist.
It hums, steady and low, beneath the drama of the moment.

Sharpening your perception requires slowing down.
It requires silence —
not just the absence of sound, but the absence of mental clutter.
It requires developing a tolerance for boredom, for emptiness, for
moments when nothing urgent happens and nothing begs for your
attention.

In these moments, the mind begins to clear.
And in the clearing, patterns emerge.

The stock market ticker scrolls endlessly with numbers and
percentages — noise to most.
But the trained observer watches not the daily fluctuations but the
underlying cycles of fear and greed that repeat like the seasons.

The news cycles spin stories out of every event — most forgotten
before the week is over.
But the signal lies in what persists, what changes slowly, what
builds pressure quietly beneath the headlines.

In conversations, too, the real message is not always in the words spoken but in the patterns of silence, the gestures, the shifts in tone that reveal the truths people are reluctant to say out loud.

Sharpening your signal-to-noise ratio is not about becoming detached or cold.
It is about becoming precise.
It is about reserving your attention for what has weight, for what repeats, for what endures after the excitement has faded.

Those who cannot filter noise live in a state of constant reaction — exhausted, scattered, confused.
Those who can filter it move differently.
They move slowly but decisively.
They wait longer, but strike with greater force.
They appear calm because they are not chasing the noise — they are following the signal.

In a culture addicted to stimulation, clarity becomes a rare and powerful advantage.

Noise will always be louder.
Signal will always be quieter.
The difference is who learns to listen to the right one.

# Practical Exercises for Pattern Recognition

Pattern recognition, like any serious discipline, does not come from inspiration.
It comes from training.

There is no moment of sudden revelation, no flash of insight that permanently changes the way you see.
There is only practice — quiet, deliberate, often invisible practice.

The work begins with slowing down.
Most people move too quickly to notice anything beyond the immediate.
They skim the surface of events and conversations, mistaking motion for observation.
To train the pattern eye, you must resist this speed.
You must become comfortable with stillness — not inactivity, but attention without rush.

It begins in simple ways.

Start by revisiting events after they happen.
Not in judgment, but in analysis.
What did I miss?
What was predictable in hindsight?
What were the early signs, the small fractures, the quiet signals that preceded the noise?

Memory becomes a laboratory.
Your past is not just a story you survived — it is raw data waiting to be re-examined.
Patterns rarely announce themselves in real time.
They reveal themselves in retrospect — but only to those willing to look.

The discipline extends into how you consume information.
Most people read quickly and widely, grazing on opinions and headlines, mistaking quantity for depth.
But the pattern eye sharpens by reading slowly, carefully, repeatedly.

Choose one topic — history, markets, psychology — and go deep instead of wide.
Read not to collect facts, but to see rhythms.
What recurs?
What fades?
What returns under a different name?

The same applies to conversations.
Most people listen to reply.
Few listen to understand.
Fewer still listen for patterns.

The next time you are in a discussion, step back from the words themselves.
Listen for the habits underneath — the unspoken assumptions, the repeated narratives, the predictable defenses.
People, like markets and empires, are governed by their patterns.
Most never see their own.

And there is the deeper exercise:
turning the eye inward.

It is one thing to recognize the patterns in others, in history, in the movements of the world.
It is another to see the patterns in yourself — the repetitions that undermine your own progress, the habits that sabotage your own intentions.

What failures do you return to, not by accident but by habit?
What conflicts find you, again and again, wearing different faces but speaking the same language?

This is the hardest work — and the most necessary.
For the eye that cannot see its own patterns is blind in the places that matter most.

Pattern recognition is not a mystical gift.
It is the reward for attention paid over time — a skill honed not in moments of excitement, but in long stretches of deliberate observation.

It is not complicated.
It is simply rare.

Because most people are too busy moving, talking, consuming, reacting.
Few are willing to sit still long enough to notice the quiet echoes beneath the noise.

But for those who do, the world begins to look different.
Less random.
Less overwhelming.

More patterned.
More navigable.

More honest.

## Seeing Beyond Immediacy — Patience as a Perceptive Tool

Immediacy is the enemy of perception.

The modern world worships the instant — instant communication, instant response, instant gratification.
It teaches impatience as a virtue.
It rewards those who react quickly, who respond first, who move fast enough to stay ahead of everyone else chasing the same distractions.

But the truth is quiet, and it is slow.
Patterns do not reveal themselves to the impatient.
They emerge only over time, for those who are willing to watch without rushing, to observe without forcing, to wait without grasping for immediate clarity.

Patience is not a passive trait.
It is not resignation or apathy.
Patience is an active state — a discipline of attention stretched over time.

It is in patience that observation deepens.
Most events look chaotic at first glance.
Markets rise and fall with no clear reason.
Relationships twist and fray seemingly overnight.
Success appears and disappears without warning.

But these are first impressions, reflections caught too early, too close.

If you step back and wait,
if you allow time to unfold without demanding it explain itself at every turn,
you begin to see what others miss.

You see that market crashes are not sudden, but the final act of years of quiet excess.
You see that personal failures are not random, but the accumulation of neglected decisions.
You see that relationships do not collapse in an instant, but through the slow erosion of trust, conversation by conversation.

Patience reveals the long arcs hidden inside short-term volatility.

Where others see only the noise of the moment, the patient mind begins to detect the rhythm underneath —
the slow build, the gradual shift, the inevitable return.

It is easy to mistake speed for progress.
It is easy to confuse motion with momentum.

But patience teaches you the difference.
It slows your eyes, your mind, your judgment,
until you can see not only what is happening,
but what is forming.

Patience is what separates the reactive from the strategic,
the frantic from the focused,
the lost from the prepared.

It is not that patient people see further into the future.
It is that they see deeper into the present.

They notice what is not yet obvious.
They trust that what is real does not need to shout to be heard.
They believe that what matters will become visible in time — and so they wait, they watch, they listen.

And in that waiting, the world unfolds itself to them.

Patience, then, is not a delay in action.
It is preparation.
It is alignment with the deeper rhythms of things — rhythms that cannot be rushed, cannot be demanded, cannot be hacked.

To train the pattern eye is to train patience.

For without patience, all you will ever see is noise.

And without patience, all you will ever do is react to it.

---

# Chapter 4
# Patterns in Business, Relationships, and Self

---

## Business Cycles — Boom, Bust, and the Myth of "This Time Is Different"

---

In business, as in nature, cycles are inevitable.
Yet each generation convinces itself that the rules have changed,
that this time is different, that the old lessons no longer apply.

It begins in periods of expansion.
Growth seems effortless.
Capital is abundant.
Optimism replaces caution.
Mistakes are hidden by momentum.
Companies scale rapidly, fueled not by discipline but by the
intoxicating belief that the cycle has been conquered.

Warnings are dismissed.
Skeptics are ridiculed.

The new era, we are told, is unprecedented — immune to the failures of the past.

But cycles do not care about sentiment.
They are indifferent to belief.

What grows too fast often grows hollow.
What rises without foundation eventually cracks.

Every business cycle follows the same familiar arc:
optimism blooms into mania,
mania tips into overreach,
overreach collapses into retreat,
retreat clears the ground for the next wave of disciplined builders.

The companies that survive are not the ones that believe the boom will last forever.
They are the ones that prepare for winter while others still celebrate summer.

They conserve resources when others spend recklessly.
They invest in foundations when others chase surface gains.
They move deliberately when others move frantically.

The myth of "this time is different" has been the prelude to every major collapse:
the dot-com bubble,
the housing crash,
the speculative excesses of industries that rise too quickly on the backs of new technologies and human impatience.

Each collapse feels sudden to those who only watched the surface.
To those who studied the patterns, it is familiar — inevitable.

The discipline of recognizing business cycles is not about predicting the exact moment of decline.
It is about understanding the structure beneath the story — the deep tide that rises and falls no matter how loudly the waves insist on their uniqueness.

It is the humility to know that cycles are stronger than optimism. And that survival, in business as in life, belongs not to the most exuberant, but to the most prepared.

---

## Relationship Patterns — Why Personal Dynamics Are Predictive

---

In relationships, as in markets, the surface often distracts from the truth.

We are taught to see relationships as unique —
each friendship, each partnership, each bond unlike any other.
And on the surface, they are: different faces, different stories, different moments of joy or disappointment.

But beneath the individuality lies something more familiar, more ancient:
the slow, repeating rhythm of human connection and disconnection.

Most relationships follow a pattern.
Attraction, attention, mutual discovery — the beginning is often effortless.

Curiosity carries the weight.
Excitement covers the imperfections.
There is grace, there is energy, there is optimism — the belief that this bond is different from all others that have come before.

But time wears away at the newness.
Habits form.
Assumptions solidify.
The very familiarity that once felt like comfort becomes a kind of blindness.
We stop seeing the other person as they are and begin seeing them as we expect them to be.
We listen less carefully.
We speak with less curiosity.
We assume.

If left unexamined, small fractures form — not from crises, but from repetition.
From the unchecked loop of misunderstanding.
From the patterns of conflict that repeat because they were never truly resolved, only postponed.
From the rituals of avoidance — the conversation that is never had, the resentment that is never named, the apology that is never truly offered.

In the early stages, these patterns are faint, like hairline cracks in a foundation.
Easy to ignore.
Easy to dismiss.

But patterns, if left unaddressed, do not stay faint.
They deepen.
They widen.
They harden into the very structure of the relationship.

By the time collapse comes — the silence, the withdrawal, the betrayal — it feels sudden.
But suddenness is an illusion born of inattentiveness.

The cracks were there all along.
They simply grew patiently while no one was looking.

The discipline of seeing relationship patterns is not about suspicion or cynicism.
It is about attentiveness.
It is the practice of noticing not just what is said, but what is repeated.
Not just what is felt, but what is rehearsed.

It is the willingness to ask, again and again:
What dynamic are we creating together?
Is this movement familiar because it is healthy, or simply because it is easy?
Are we building something, or are we repeating something we already know how to destroy?

The dynamics we fall into most easily are rarely the healthiest.
They are the most practiced.
They are the ones we learned early, often without realizing it — the scripts handed down by families, by past friendships, by the failures we have yet to name.

Seeing relationship patterns requires humility.
It requires the courage to recognize that the conflict is rarely about the surface argument.
It is about the rhythm underneath — the needs unspoken, the wounds unhealed, the habits unchallenged.

Those who cannot see these patterns are doomed to repeat them — not just with one person, but with every person they allow close.

Those who can see them, who can name them, who can sit in the discomfort of truth long enough to break them —
those people build relationships that endure not because they are free from difficulty, but because they are free from blindness.

Patterns do not dictate the future.
But they predict it, unless we interrupt them.

And interruption, in relationships as in life, begins with attention.

---

## Self-Patterns — Habits, Failures, and the Stories We Repeat

---

The most difficult patterns to see are not the ones in markets or relationships.
They are the ones in ourselves.

It is easy to study external cycles — easier still to observe the behaviors of others.
But to sit quietly and trace the outlines of your own life is a harder discipline.

Yet the patterns are there, unmistakable for anyone willing to look.

We move through life repeating certain stories.
We frame ourselves as the hero, the victim, the outsider, the misunderstood.
And without realizing it, we build habits that fulfill the role we have cast ourselves in.

We chase similar dreams and collide with similar disappointments.
We sabotage opportunities in familiar ways.
We nurture the same doubts, replay the same failures, circle the same fears — not because life conspires against us, but because we conspire against ourselves without knowing it.

The habits of thought are the deepest grooves.
They are not loud.
They do not announce their presence.
They hum in the background, shaping decisions quietly, efficiently.

The person who doubts their worth will find ways to undercut their success —
not all at once, but incrementally, invisibly.
The person who fears abandonment will sabotage connection before it has the chance to deepen.
The person addicted to urgency will stay forever busy, forever scattered, never resting long enough to confront the deeper work that cannot be rushed.

We repeat because repetition is familiar.
And familiarity, even when painful, feels safer than the unknown.

It is not fate.
It is habit — unconscious, practiced over years, reinforced by avoidance.

The challenge is not merely to see these patterns once, in a moment of clarity.
It is to see them continually, to recognize their shapes each time they try to reassert themselves, to refuse the easy comfort of the known mistake.

It requires a kind of double vision —
the ability to live your life while simultaneously observing it,
the ability to act while remaining aware of the old scripts trying to direct the action.

Self-patterns are not always destructive.
Some habits, once noticed, can be reworked, reshaped.
Some cycles, once interrupted, can become spiral — not endless circles, but slow upward turns.

But the first move is not change.
The first move is awareness.

It is sitting with the discomfort of recognition:
the realization that the problems we blame on luck or circumstance often carry our fingerprints.

It is noticing where our own hands are on the wheel, even when we would rather believe otherwise.

This is not about guilt.
It is about ownership.
It is about reclaiming the possibility of change from the inertia of repetition.

The patterns that define your life will either be those you name and alter,
or those you refuse to see and are enslaved by.

What you cannot see, you cannot change.
What you refuse to confront, you are doomed to repeat.

And no matter how much you achieve, no matter how fast you move,
you will carry these patterns with you —
into your work, into your relationships, into the mirror each morning —
until you are willing to stop, to study, and to choose something different.

Awareness is the beginning.
It is always the beginning.

---

# Cross-Disciplinary Pattern Recognition — Thinking Like a Generalist

---

There is a certain kind of mind that thrives in the narrow.
The specialist, the expert, the technician — trained to master the deep well of a single discipline.
Their world is precise, their language technical, their authority clear within the walls of their field.

But pattern recognition does not belong solely to the specialist.
In fact, it rarely flourishes there.
Specialization sharpens knowledge, but it can also narrow vision.
It tempts the mind to believe that the patterns of one field are the only patterns that matter.

The generalist sees differently.
They stand at the intersection of disciplines, gathering echoes from distant fields, tracing connections where others see only division.
They understand that patterns are not confined by industry, by culture, by time.

The boom-bust cycle of financial markets mirrors the rise and fall of civilizations.
The failure modes of companies resemble the slow erosion of trust in personal relationships.
The laws of ecosystems — growth, competition, collapse, regeneration — map onto human systems with eerie consistency.

The generalist trains their eye across these boundaries.
They are less interested in depth without breadth, and more interested in the structures that endure across contexts.

When they study history, they do not memorize dates; they observe rhythms of power, rebellion, decay.
When they study psychology, they look beyond theories to the ancient, repeated instincts that drive human behavior.
When they read about technology, they do not fixate on the newness but on how every tool reshapes power, alters connection, reorganizes society.

The generalist is a pattern collector, a translator between worlds.

They understand that insight often comes not from digging deeper into what you know,
but from stepping sideways into what you do not —
and recognizing that the same currents flow there too, only in different language, different forms.

Innovation, despite its myth, is rarely the product of pure invention.
It is often the product of borrowing — taking a solution from one domain and applying it to a problem in another.

The architect who studies music finds new rhythms in the design of space.
The scientist who studies philosophy frames better questions, not just better experiments.
The leader who studies biology leads organizations with an understanding of adaptation, not just command.

Pattern recognition grows sharper when it is exercised across domains.
The broader your lens, the more subtle the echoes you can hear.

But this breadth does not come easily.
It requires humility — the willingness to be a beginner again and again, to enter unfamiliar fields without the armor of expertise.
It requires patience — the discipline to study slowly, to read widely, to synthesize rather than simply accumulate.

It requires living with questions longer than most are comfortable, holding contradictions without rushing to resolve them,
seeing not the differences between things, but the underlying structures they share.

Generalists are not immune to mistakes.
But they are less vulnerable to narrow blindness.
They are less likely to mistake the map for the territory,
less likely to be seduced by the illusion that the patterns of their field are the patterns of the world.

In a time obsessed with specialization, generalists are often underestimated.

But they are also often the ones who see the break before it happens,
who anticipate the shift before it becomes obvious,
who adapt faster when change demands not deeper expertise but broader vision.

Pattern recognition belongs to those who are willing to move between worlds —
to those who understand that while the vocabulary may change, the grammar of reality remains the same.

---

## How Fluency in Patterns Compounds Over Time

---

There are skills that grow through repetition — muscle memory, reflex, habit.
And then there are skills that grow through accumulation — slow, deliberate layering over time,
not in visible leaps but in silent depths.

Pattern recognition belongs to the second kind.

It compounds quietly.
Each observation builds on the last.
Each recognition sharpens the lens a little further.
Each mistake, properly examined, feeds the next cycle of awareness.

At first, the practice feels slow, even invisible.
You notice a pattern, but not always soon enough to act on it.
You recognize a cycle, but not yet with enough clarity to intervene.
You see the signs, but hesitate, unsure if they are real or imagined.

But slowly — so slowly it escapes notice — something changes.
The eye sharpens.
The mind quickens.
The noise fades faster.
The signal surfaces sooner.

You begin to see the familiar structures behind unfamiliar faces.
You hear the old rhythms playing inside new headlines.
You recognize the slight tension before the collapse,
the flicker of instability before the fall.

Patterns that once seemed faint become clear.
Situations that once seemed random reveal their structure.
The world, which once looked chaotic, begins to show its scaffolding.

And with each recognition, your ability deepens — not linearly,
but exponentially.

Fluency compounds.

It builds not just knowledge, but instinct.
A kind of silent readiness — not certainty, but orientation.
You know how cycles begin, how they mature, how they decay.
You know where mistakes cluster.
You know how success blinds, how decline whispers before it shouts.

This fluency does not protect you from every failure.
It does not grant invincibility.

But it grants something better — resilience.
The ability to see setbacks in context, not isolation.
The ability to move through cycles, not be broken by them.

With time, the compound effect of fluency creates distance.
While others react impulsively, you move deliberately.
While others are surprised by the inevitable, you are prepared for the possible.
While others are trapped by their patterns, you are free to alter yours.

The mind that has accumulated patterns over years sees differently.
Not faster, but deeper.
Not louder, but clearer.

In a world that celebrates speed, fluency rewards patience.
It honors those willing to move slowly enough to understand what is really happening —
and quietly enough to act before the obvious becomes obvious.

Fluency in patterns is not a moment of mastery.
It is a lifetime of attention, compounding invisibly,
until what was once rare becomes second nature.

The best see it.
The rest, still distracted by noise, call it luck.

# Chapter 5
# Avoiding False Patterns

## Overfitting — The Danger of Seeing Patterns That Aren't Real

Not every rhythm is a pattern.
Not every coincidence is a signal.
Not every repetition is a truth.

The mind, once trained to notice patterns, faces a new danger —
the temptation to see them where they do not exist.

This is the danger of overfitting —
the art of connecting dots that are not meant to be connected,
of drawing conclusions from noise,
of mistaking randomness for rhythm.

It is the trap of seeing order where there is only accident,
of creating narratives to explain what needs no explanation
beyond chance.

Overfitting is not a mistake of stupidity.
It is a mistake of overconfidence, of an intelligence too eager to impose meaning on the meaningless.

In markets, it appears as the trader who believes they have unlocked the secret pattern behind price movements —
who convinces themselves that the last three cycles predict the next,
only to find that the market does not care about their charts.

In relationships, it is the lover who sees betrayal in every silence,
who traces old wounds onto new faces,
mistaking fear for foresight, mistaking ghosts for warnings.

In life, it is the person who believes every misfortune is a message,
every coincidence a conspiracy,
every failure a sign that the universe has singled them out.

The danger of overfitting is that it feels like insight.
It flatters the mind with the illusion of mastery.
It tells us we are seeing deeper than others —
when in truth, we are only weaving stories out of random threads.

Real patterns are disciplined.
They emerge over time, across contexts, with enough consistency to endure scrutiny.

False patterns crumble under pressure.
They collapse when examined from different angles.
They dissolve when tested against new information.

But the mind, once enchanted by a false pattern, resists letting go.
It prefers certainty to uncertainty, even if that certainty is an illusion.

The disciplined observer must cultivate a kind of humility —
the willingness to admit that not every repetition carries meaning,
that not every movement is a sign,
that some things happen for no reason at all.

To avoid overfitting is not to abandon the search for patterns.
It is to temper it.
It is to remember that wisdom lies not just in seeing, but in
knowing when not to see.

It is the art of leaving some questions unanswered,
some noise unfiltered,
some dots unconnected.

Because true understanding is not found in the desperate search
for meaning,
but in the patient acceptance of uncertainty.

The world is not obligated to make sense on our terms.
It moves to rhythms deeper and wilder than we can predict.

Sometimes, the most powerful act of perception is restraint —
the ability to step back, to resist the impulse to explain,
to let some mysteries remain mysteries.

In a mind sharpened by patience and humility,
real patterns emerge more clearly —
not because they are forced,
but because they are found.

# Randomness, Luck, and Noise — Knowing the Difference

Much of what happens in life is not pattern.
It is randomness.

But the mind resists this truth.
It longs for meaning, for narrative, for reasons behind every rise
and every fall.
It struggles to accept that luck — pure, indifferent, chaotic luck
— plays a far greater role than we care to admit.

Randomness does not flatter the ego.
It offers no storyline where we are the heroes of our own design.
It humbles, reminding us that we are often passengers, not pilots.

Yet to live well — to think clearly — is to make peace with
randomness.
It is to understand that not every victory is earned, not every
defeat deserved,
that not every success is the fruit of wisdom, nor every failure the
proof of stupidity.

Randomness governs far more than we realize —
the timing of an introduction, the conditions of a market,
the unseen variables that tilt one life toward abundance and
another toward hardship.

Luck is not a strategy.
It cannot be summoned or controlled.
But it must be acknowledged.
Because mistaking luck for pattern leads to arrogance —
the belief that what has worked once will always work,
the illusion that outcomes are always the result of inputs.

The world is noisier than we admit.
Information comes wrapped in layers of distortion,
trends appear where none exist,
apparent signals shimmer and disappear under scrutiny.

The disciplined mind learns to distinguish between noise and
signal, between pattern and accident.
It does not seek certainty in every coincidence.
It does not build meaning on foundations of randomness.
It recognizes that much of what is celebrated as genius is luck
wearing the mask of inevitability.

This is not a call to fatalism.
It is a call to humility.
It is an invitation to act wisely within a world where control is
limited and randomness ever-present.

To know the difference between randomness and pattern is to
move with a different kind of strength —
the strength of resilience rather than prediction,
the strength of preparation rather than prophecy.

It is the understanding that while you cannot command luck,
you can shape your habits, your resilience, your readiness —
so that when luck tilts in your favor, you are prepared to seize it,
and when it does not, you are prepared to endure it.

Noise will always exist.
Randomness will always swirl around intention.
Luck will always dance just beyond control.

The wise do not waste their lives trying to capture the wind.
They set their sails, adjust with the currents,
and move forward —
not because they command the forces around them,
but because they have learned to navigate them.

---

## Cognitive Biases That Manufacture False Signals

---

The mind does not merely stumble upon false patterns.
It manufactures them.

It is not simply that we are surrounded by noise and randomness
—

it is that we are wired to interpret noise as signal, to invent order
where none exists, to build stories out of fragments.

This is not a flaw in some of us.
It is a feature of all of us.

Cognitive biases — the invisible distortions of thought — are not
rare exceptions.
They are the default settings of the human mind.

Confirmation bias urges us to see what we already believe,
filtering out contradictions, highlighting supporting evidence,
building castles of certainty on foundations of selective memory.

Patternicity — the tendency to perceive patterns in random data
—
tricks us into connecting the stars, drawing constellations from
chaos.
We see faces in clouds, omens in accidents, significance in
coincidence.

The clustering illusion convinces us that random events are not
random —
that streaks in gambling, strings of successes, runs of failures
must mean something, must reveal a deeper order.

Hindsight bias smooths the rough edges of the past,
convincing us that what has happened was always bound to
happen —
that the patterns were obvious all along, that we would have seen
them if only we had looked harder.

The mind, restless and proud, cannot tolerate uncertainty.
It rushes to complete pictures, to resolve ambiguity, to find
answers even when no answers exist.

And so it invents.

It draws patterns where there are none.
It reads meaning into noise.
It mistakes accident for design.

The danger is not merely personal.
Entire markets move on the illusions crafted by collective biases.
Entire industries rise and fall on narratives built from wishful
thinking and selective perception.

Entire nations chart courses on stories woven from the threads of fear and pride.

Awareness of bias is not immunity from bias.
Even those who study these distortions are not free from them.
But awareness is a beginning.

It slows the mind's rush to certainty.
It introduces hesitation where arrogance would leap forward.
It invites questions where the mind would prefer quick answers.

What if the pattern I see is not real?
What if I am weaving meaning where there is only noise?
What if the story I am telling myself is a story I need to believe, not a truth the world is offering?

The disciplined mind is not free from bias.
But it is familiar with its own distortions.
It knows the mind's hunger for meaning, its discomfort with randomness, its weakness for stories that flatter and reassure.

And so it moves cautiously,
testing its perceptions,
challenging its conclusions,
remaining suspicious of clarity that comes too easily.

In a world drowning in information,
the real skill is not to find patterns everywhere —
it is to resist the mind's impulse to fabricate them.

It is to stand still while others sprint toward false certainty,
to listen longer,
to doubt more generously,
to understand that not every thread leads to a tapestry,
not every coincidence hides a message.

The mind will always manufacture false signals.
Wisdom lies not in eliminating this tendency,
but in learning to doubt what feels most certain.

Because certainty, more often than not, is the surest sign that we
have been deceived —
not by the world,
but by ourselves.

---

# When Pattern Recognition Becomes Paranoia

---

There is a fine line between vigilance and fear,
between wisdom and obsession.

Pattern recognition, if left unchecked, can slip quietly into its
shadow form —
paranoia.

The mind trained to notice connections may begin to see
connections everywhere,
even where none exist.
The discipline of careful observation becomes the burden of
constant suspicion.
The skill that once clarified the world now clouds it.

Paranoia is not simply caution magnified.
It is the corruption of perception itself.
It is the conviction that every coincidence carries threat,

that every movement hides malice,
that every unexplained event conceals intention.

The paranoid mind does not seek patterns to understand the world.
It seeks them to defend against it.
It assembles meaning not to navigate reality more skillfully,
but to protect itself from imagined dangers.

In its grip, every silence is sinister.
Every delay, a warning.
Every deviation, a betrayal.

It is not the absence of evidence that defines paranoia —
it is the refusal to accept uncertainty.
It is the demand that everything must have an explanation,
and that every explanation must confirm the worst.

Paranoia masquerades as pattern recognition,
but it violates the fundamental discipline at the heart of true observation:
patience.

Paranoia rushes to judgment.
It insists on conclusions before the evidence is ready to speak.
It fills in blanks with fear, weaves narratives from absence,
prefers a wrong answer to no answer at all.

And once the mind falls into paranoia, it becomes a closed loop.
Evidence against the fear is dismissed as deception.
Contradictions are not corrections; they are further proof of the conspiracy.

In business, this mindset destroys trust —
leaders who see betrayal in every disagreement,

companies that retreat into fear and suspicion,
teams paralyzed by the belief that every risk conceals sabotage.

In relationships, it corrodes intimacy —
partners who interrogate rather than converse,
friends who vanish under the weight of imagined slights.

In the self, it becomes a prison —
a life lived under siege,
where the greatest danger is no longer the world outside,
but the mind's own relentless invention of threats.

The antidote to paranoia is not blindness.
It is humility.
It is the willingness to live with uncertainty,
to admit that not everything can be explained,
that not every event carries a hidden agenda,
that the absence of information is not evidence of danger.

Pattern recognition, rightly practiced, demands patience.
It requires the discipline to wait, to gather, to test, to question —
to sit with not knowing, without rushing to fabricate a knowing
that only deepens ignorance.

It is not a sign of weakness to admit uncertainty.
It is a sign of strength —
the strength to hold complexity without collapsing into fear,
the strength to move forward without the crutch of false certainty.

Paranoia offers the illusion of control.
Pattern recognition offers the reality of understanding.
And reality, for all its difficulty, is always the better companion.

# How to Build a Filter — Skepticism Without Cynicism

In a world overflowing with information and misdirection,
the mind must develop a filter.

Not a wall —
not the hard, defensive posture of cynicism that rejects
everything,
but a finer instrument —
one that lets the true through and keeps the false at bay.

Skepticism, properly understood, is not doubt turned bitter.
It is doubt turned disciplined.

It is the habit of questioning without dismissing,
of testing without attacking,
of slowing down the rush to judgment without falling into
paralysis.

The mind that lacks skepticism is gullible,
tossed from certainty to certainty by every trend, every noise,
every seeming pattern.
But the mind that drowns in cynicism loses something equally
vital —
the ability to believe, to trust, to engage.

Cynicism is lazy skepticism.
It protects itself not by discernment, but by rejection.

It assumes the worst not because it has tested reality,
but because it is unwilling to risk being wrong.

True skepticism risks being wrong.
It listens.
It questions.
It waits.
It tests.

It understands that patterns exist —
but it also understands that not every movement, not every connection,
deserves to be elevated into a truth.

Building a filter begins with patience.
It begins with the discipline to delay conclusions,
to let events unfold,
to seek corroboration instead of validation,
to gather enough data that the pattern, if it exists, reveals itself
without needing to be forced.

The skeptic asks:
What is the evidence?
What are the alternatives?
What might I be missing?
Where might my own desires or fears be distorting what I see?

The cynic assumes:
Nothing is true.
Nothing is good.
Nothing can be trusted.

But skepticism keeps the door open —
open enough to let truth in,
closed enough to keep delusion out.

It is a practice of balance —
to see the world clearly without becoming hardened by it,
to recognize deception without losing the capacity for belief,
to notice the patterns without seeing conspiracy in every
coincidence.

In leadership, skepticism protects decisions from the impulsive
certainty of noise,
but preserves the openness needed for vision.
In relationships, it guards trust without poisoning it,
allowing loyalty to grow in the soil of reality rather than fantasy.

In the self, skepticism builds resilience —
an ability to question one's own judgments,
to revise, to rethink, to admit error without collapse.

The filter is not perfect.
No mind, however disciplined, is immune to mistakes.
But without it, the mind is defenseless —
a hollow vessel filled by the loudest voice,
the nearest pattern,
the easiest lie.

Skepticism is an art.
It is the art of believing carefully,
of loving carefully,
of living carefully —
without surrendering to fear,
without retreating into despair.

It is a way of moving through a noisy, complicated world —
alert, aware, awake —
eyes open not just to what is there,
but to what is not.

The skeptic listens longer.
Waits longer.
Watches longer.

And in the waiting, sees more.

---

# Chapter 6
# Why Relationships Break Under Business Logic

## The Tyranny of Efficiency — How It Ruins Human Bonds

Efficiency is a virtue in business.
It trims waste.
It accelerates outcomes.
It optimizes every process for maximum output at minimum cost.

But what serves the machine does not always serve the human.
And when the logic of efficiency invades our relationships,
it does not sharpen them.
It hollows them out.

Efficiency thrives on speed, clarity, predictability.
Human bonds, by contrast, thrive on patience, ambiguity, and mess.

The logic of efficiency asks:
What do I get from this?

How fast can I get it?
How little can I give to receive what I want?

It demands results.
It expects returns.
It calculates worth based on visible output.

But relationships are not transactions.
They do not yield to metrics.
They resist being streamlined, optimized, reduced to input and output.

The strongest relationships are not efficient.
They are redundant, filled with rituals that serve no practical function —
the repeated conversations, the unhurried meals, the unnecessary kindnesses.

They are inefficient in their demands —
requiring forgiveness without timelines,
attention without agendas,
care without calculation.

When efficiency becomes the guiding principle of how we treat others,
we lose the very elements that make connection possible.
We strip away the slow, unproductive moments where trust is built,
where loyalty is tested,
where understanding deepens.

We begin to measure people by what they can deliver,
by how smoothly they fit into our plans,
by how little friction they cause in our carefully scheduled lives.

And when they fail to meet those expectations — as inevitably they must —
we discard them,
the way a machine discards a part that no longer functions.

Efficiency cannot tolerate the messiness of real friendship,
the slow work of real love,
the unpredictable unfolding of real loyalty.

It demands control.
But trust is built on surrender.
It demands speed.
But intimacy grows slowly.
It demands certainty.
But real connection lives in vulnerability, in the spaces where guarantees are impossible.

The tyranny of efficiency promises that we can have relationships without their costs —
without the inconvenience, the misunderstanding, the forgiveness, the waiting.
But this promise is a lie.

Relationships do not break because people stop caring.
They break because the slow, inefficient rituals that sustain care are abandoned in favor of productivity,
because the logic of the ledger replaces the logic of loyalty.

A relationship optimized for efficiency is not a relationship.
It is a contract.
And contracts are not built for love.

The habits that build real connection are not scalable.
They are not productive.
They are not efficient.

They are wasteful in the best possible way.

They waste time.
They waste attention.
They waste energy.

And in that waste, they build something that no machine, no system, no business model can replicate.

Something that lasts.

---

## Why Relationships Don't Respond to Optimization

---

Optimization is a powerful tool when the goal is efficiency.
When the aim is to produce more with less,
to cut waste, to refine process, to deliver faster,
optimization is a kind of silent genius —
a force that makes the complex smoother, the slow faster, the costly cheaper.

But what optimization serves in systems,
it suffocates in relationships.

Relationships are not systems.
They are living organisms.
They cannot be engineered into perfection.
They cannot be optimized without being diminished.

To optimize something is to strip it of excess,
to smooth its rough edges,
to make it predictable, scalable, controllable.

But love, friendship, loyalty —
they live in the excess.
They live in the unpredictable.
They live in the spaces optimization would call inefficient,
unnecessary, irrelevant.

You cannot optimize friendship by removing misunderstanding.
You cannot optimize love by eliminating difficulty.
You cannot optimize loyalty by ensuring it is never tested.

Real relationships respond not to refinement, but to resilience.
Not to control, but to surrender.
Not to efficiency, but to care that lingers, even when it is
inconvenient.

Optimization asks:
How can we remove the friction?

But friction is not the enemy in a relationship.
Friction is the place where growth happens.
It is the place where differences surface,
where forgiveness is practiced,
where the true work of intimacy begins.

Optimization asks:
How can we guarantee the outcome?

But relationships live in uncertainty.
They require trust without guarantees,
faith without certainty.

Optimization asks:
How can we scale this?

But relationships do not scale.
They are built slowly, carefully, individually —
one conversation, one failure, one act of patience at a time.

To treat a relationship as a system to be optimized
is to misunderstand its nature completely.

It is to confuse depth with convenience,
to trade slow trust for fast transaction,
to reduce the sacred to the functional.

People are not products.
Connections are not commodities.
Care cannot be rushed, and it cannot be streamlined.

What matters in relationships is often invisible —
the moments when no one is counting,
the gifts given without expectation,
the forgiveness offered without negotiation.

Optimization cannot measure these things.
It cannot quantify grace.
It cannot standardize presence.
It cannot predict loyalty.

The relationships that endure — the ones that matter —
are not those that have been optimized for ease.
They are the ones that have survived inconvenience, difficulty,
and mess,
and have been made stronger for it.

In a world obsessed with faster, cheaper, better,
the real luxury is slowness.

The real success is presence.
The real wealth is loyalty that was not earned through transaction,
but forged through the inefficiencies of real care.

Relationships do not respond to optimization.
They respond to attention.
To patience.
To the kind of presence that wastes time without apology.

To the kind of love that cannot be measured,
only lived.

---

# The Fallacy of Transactional Living

---

We are taught early, and often, that life is a transaction.

Give value. Get value.
Offer something. Expect something in return.
Relationships are framed as exchanges —
time for attention, care for loyalty, service for love.

And beneath it all, a quiet arithmetic:
What am I getting for what I am giving?

At first glance, this seems rational.
Fair, even.
No one wants to give endlessly and receive nothing.
No one wants to be taken for granted.

But transactional living, when it becomes the hidden operating system of a relationship, corrodes it from within.
Not because exchange is wrong — but because real connection is not built on balance sheets.

When every interaction becomes a silent negotiation,
when every gift must be matched,
when every kindness demands a return,
something essential is lost.

Grace disappears.
Spontaneity withers.
Trust — which cannot survive the constant auditing of intentions — begins to erode.

Love cannot be bargained.
Friendship cannot be traded.
Loyalty cannot be calculated.

They must be given freely,
not because the return is guaranteed,
but because the giving itself is the point.

Transactional living promises clarity —
You know where you stand.
You know what you owe and what you are owed.

But it delivers something colder:
relationships stripped of wonder,
connections reduced to contracts,
people measured not by who they are, but by what they provide.

It teaches you to ask the wrong questions:
Not — *Is this relationship true?*
But — *Is this relationship profitable?*

Not — *Am I present?*
But — *Am I getting enough back?*

Transactional living builds relationships that are efficient, fair,
and empty.
They last only as long as the balance remains favorable,
only as long as the transaction remains smooth.

The moment life becomes difficult —
when one side cannot give as much, when the returns are delayed
or diminished —
these relationships fracture.
Because without the transaction, there is nothing left.

Real relationships endure because they are built on something
deeper —
on a loyalty that survives imbalance,
on a love that persists through seasons of uneven giving,
on a friendship that can absorb the temporary unfairness that real
life demands.

There is no lasting bond that is always equal.
No lasting love that is always reciprocal.
No lasting friendship that keeps strict accounts.

The fallacy of transactional living is that it looks stable —
as long as everything is measured, everything will remain fair.

But life is not fair.
And fairness is not the soil where loyalty grows.
The soil is grace.
The soil is forgiveness.
The soil is patience.

The relationships that endure — the ones that nourish, that
sustain, that hold us up when life bends us low —
are not built on transactions.

They are built on the quiet decision, made again and again,
to give even when the return is uncertain,
to stay even when staying costs more than it repays,
to care even when care is inconvenient.

In the end, transactional living trades away what matters most —
and buys only what cannot last.

---

# Human Dynamics as Nonlinear, Messy, and Beautiful

---

We are trained to prefer the linear.
The straight line.
The clear progression.
The neat chart with its tidy, upward slope.

Linear feels safe.
Predictable.
It promises that if we input the right effort, at the right time, in the
right way, we will get the right result.

But human beings do not move in straight lines.
We loop.
We spiral.
We regress.

We leap forward unpredictably and fall backward without warning.

Human dynamics are not linear.
They are wild and nonlinear, shaped by emotion, history, memory, fear, hope —
forces that cannot be graphed or forecasted with any real precision.

A friendship deepens not in a steady climb,
but in sudden moments —
an unexpected confession,
an act of forgiveness,
a silent hour spent together when words fail.

Love matures not by ticking milestones off a list,
but by surviving storms,
by finding tenderness after anger,
by discovering loyalty after disappointment.

Families fracture and heal along invisible lines.
Old wounds surface.
New trust is born.
Progress does not come in tidy increments —
it comes in bursts and pauses, surges and retreats.

It is messy.
And it is beautiful.

Because what grows in straight lines is not alive.
It is manufactured.
It is engineered.

Life, real life, grows in curves, in jagged paths,
in cycles that do not consult our plans.

To demand that relationships move neatly from one phase to the next —
to insist on constant progress, perpetual harmony, uninterrupted alignment —
is to misunderstand what they are.

It is to mistake the living for the mechanical.

The business mind craves metrics.
The human heart craves meaning.

And meaning is rarely found in the clean, the perfect, the optimized.
It is found in the unplanned resilience of a friendship that bends but does not break,
in the jagged beauty of a love that survives disappointment,
in the patient weaving of trust across years of mistake and forgiveness.

The world will offer you systems that promise linear improvement:
Follow these steps.
Hit these milestones.
Earn these rewards.

But human connection refuses to be reduced to steps or milestones.
It blooms unevenly, grows unpredictably, defies easy measures of success.

The moments that matter most —
you will not see them coming.
You will not plan for them.
They will not arrive on schedule.

They will arrive in the pauses between plans,
in the mistakes you survive together,
in the slow, patient accumulation of presence and care.

To love another person is not to manage them like a project.
It is to walk with them, unsure of the path,
trusting not in certainty, but in willingness.

The willingness to stay.
The willingness to forgive.
The willingness to begin again.

Human dynamics are nonlinear, messy, and — because of this —
they are beautiful.

Not in spite of the mess.
But because of it.

---

# Chapter 7
# The Metrics of the Heart

---

## Why the Most Important Things Can't Be Measured

---

There is a comfort in measurement.
A reassurance in numbers.
They promise objectivity, clarity, control.

You can track your revenue, your miles run, your hours worked, your deals closed.
You can plot them on a graph and tell yourself a story of progress
—
an upward climb, a line of improvement, a clear return on effort.

But the most important things resist this clarity.
They do not plot easily on charts.
They do not fit into spreadsheets.
They cannot be captured by metrics.

There is no reliable unit for trust.
No formula for loyalty.
No algorithm for forgiveness.

No quantifiable measure for the quiet, stubborn persistence of love across years of disappointment and change.

The heart refuses to be measured.
It gives no quarterly reports.
It offers no predictable returns.
It does not reward efficiency.
It rewards presence.

What matters most in life happens slowly, invisibly, often in ways we do not understand until much later —
if at all.

You cannot measure the value of a conversation that saves a friendship.
You cannot calculate the worth of a moment of grace that repairs a broken bond.
You cannot quantify the hours spent sitting quietly beside someone who needed your presence more than your words.

These things do not announce themselves as achievements.
They leave no data trail.
They offer no guarantees.
And yet they are the things that make life bearable —
and beautiful.

The modern mind, trained by business and technology, resists this.
It wants metrics for everything.
It wants to optimize even the human soul.

But to live only by what can be measured is to live a narrow, impoverished life.
It is to mistake the visible for the valuable, the quantifiable for the meaningful.

It is to miss the slow, patient accumulation of trust.
The fragile, uneven building of love.
The unremarkable acts of loyalty that, over time, weave the only
kind of wealth that cannot be lost when markets crash or titles
fade.

We chase the metrics because they are easy to understand.
But what matters most is not easy, not measurable, not tidy.
It is complicated, slow, human.

You cannot measure devotion.
You cannot predict loyalty.
You cannot force love to fit into rows and columns.

The heart has its own economy —
one that values things the world ignores,
one that rewards what cannot be scaled or rushed.

And it is in this invisible economy that life finds its real wealth.

Not in what is counted.
But in what is kept —
quietly, stubbornly, fiercely —
in the spaces that numbers cannot touch.

# Trust, Loyalty, and Love — Why They Resist Metrics

Trust is not a transaction.
It cannot be earned in units or stored in reserves.
It grows in shadows, in the unnoticed spaces between moments
—

in the pause before a reply,
in the silence after a mistake,
in the way one person stays when it would have been easier to leave.

Loyalty, too, refuses calculation.
It is not a ledger balanced by favors returned or debts repaid.
It does not tally wins or track losses.
It is the decision — made again and again in the quiet —
to remain faithful to someone even when no advantage can be gained.

And love —
love least of all submits to metrics.
It does not yield to measurement, prediction, or control.
It will not be optimized, rushed, or secured by contract.
It grows unevenly, unpredictably, often inconveniently,
out of small acts of grace that the world is too busy to notice.

These are the most powerful forces in human life —
and they resist all attempts to be counted.

We are trained to believe that what cannot be measured does not exist,
that what cannot be proven is not real.
But the deepest realities are often the most invisible.

You cannot measure the weight of a promise kept in silence.
You cannot quantify the cost of forgiveness when betrayal has been deep.
You cannot chart the distance traveled by two people who have learned, slowly, painfully, to trust each other again after trust was broken.

Trust builds in layers, over years, with no guarantee that it will last.
Loyalty is tested not in grand gestures, but in the slow erosion of convenience —
in the seasons when standing beside someone gains you nothing.

Love is not a surge of emotion,
but a long obedience in the same direction,
a thousand small decisions to care when it would be easier not to.

Metrics cannot capture these movements.
They are too slow.
Too fragile.
Too human.

The mind shaped by business logic recoils from this.
It wants guarantees, projections, assurances.
It wants to know: If I invest this much, what will I get back?
How fast?
How securely?

But the heart does not deal in guarantees.
It deals in risk —

the risk of giving with no promise of return,
the risk of trusting with no assurance of safety,
the risk of loving without knowing whether love will be returned
or rejected.

This is why the heart's metrics are so difficult —
and so necessary.

Because the things that cannot be measured are often the only
things worth giving.
The only things that survive the erosion of time.
The only things that make the uncertainty of life not just tolerable,
but worthwhile.

Trust, loyalty, love —
they resist metrics because they belong to a different economy —
an economy of grace, of patience, of risk without guarantee.

And it is only in this economy that anything truly human endures.

---

## The Hidden Balance Sheet — What's Actually Accumulating

---

There is a balance sheet in every life —
but it is not the one the world keeps.

It does not record profits or titles.
It does not count followers, promotions, or the applause of
crowds.

It is hidden, silent, ignored —
and it measures a different kind of wealth.

This balance sheet does not tally what you have earned.
It tracks what you have given.
Not what you have acquired, but what you have endured.
Not what you have won, but what you have kept faith with, even
when the world told you to let go.

Every unseen act of loyalty.
Every forgiveness no one else noticed.
Every kindness that cost you more than it benefited you.
These are the entries on the real balance sheet.

It accumulates slowly.
There are no quarterly reports, no trending graphs.
There is only the quiet, stubborn growth of a life built on things
that do not fluctuate with markets,
that do not erode with fame,
that do not disappear when fortune changes.

You cannot show this balance sheet to others.
It is not designed to impress.
It is not designed for display.

But it is real.
And it matters more than the balance sheets the world celebrates.

Because at the end of a career, a fortune, a reputation —
what remains?

Not the numbers.
Not the metrics.

What remains are the people who trust you when you have
nothing left to give them.

The ones who remember the loyalty you offered when it cost you everything.
The ones who know, even if you never said it out loud, that you could be counted on when it mattered.

What remains are the invisible investments —
the small, slow deposits made daily into the accounts of love and trust and loyalty.

These investments do not yield immediate returns.
They do not compound in ways that are visible to the impatient.

But over time, they build a kind of wealth that cannot be stolen, cannot be lost, cannot be measured —
only lived.

The hidden balance sheet is not concerned with how fast you rose.
It is concerned with how you treated people when you had the chance to exploit them and chose not to.
It is concerned with whether you loved when it was easier to walk away.
It is concerned with whether you stayed true when no one was keeping score.

Most people live as if the visible balance sheet is all that matters.
But when the lights fade, when the noise quiets, when the trophies gather dust,
it is the hidden balance sheet that will tell the real story of a life.

And it will tell it without numbers.
It will tell it through the memories others carry of you.
Through the loyalty you inspired.
Through the trust you honored.
Through the love you gave when it was neither easy nor efficient.

This is what is actually accumulating.

Even now.
Even in the silence.
Even when you cannot see it.

---

## Measuring a Life by What You Give, Not What You Get

The world teaches you to measure your life by accumulation.
By what you earn.
By what you control.
By what you gather around you as proof that you have succeeded.

But the real measure of a life is not what you get.
It is what you give.

This is not sentimentality.
It is reality, observed across the sweep of time.
The lives that echo beyond their years are not the ones filled with the most trophies,
but the ones marked by the most generous acts —
the teacher who believed in a student no one else noticed,
the friend who stood by someone when it was no longer convenient,
the parent who loved patiently, fiercely, in ways that words could never fully capture.

Getting feels powerful.
It feels like winning.
It feels like control.

But getting is always temporary.
It is vulnerable to time, to change, to the accidents of fate.

What you get can be taken away.
What you give endures.

Because what you give does not stay with you.
It moves outward —
into the lives of others,
into the memories they carry,
into the ways they move through the world because of what you gave.

The truth is brutal and simple:
You will be forgotten.
Your name will fade.
Your possessions will pass to others, then to others still, until no one remembers they were ever yours.

But what you gave —
the courage you lent to a friend,
the dignity you restored to a stranger,
the hope you ignited in someone who had begun to lose it —
these things ripple outward.

Long after your name is gone,
your giving remains,
living invisibly in places you will never see,
shaping lives you will never know.

This is the metric of the heart:
Not how much you accumulated,
but how much you spent —
spent not on consumption, but on compassion,

not on status, but on service,
not on hoarding, but on healing.

It is a quieter measure.
It will not impress the world.
It will not trend.
It will not shout your achievements to the sky.

But it will matter.
Deeply.
Permanently.

Because the currency of a life is not money, or fame, or success.
It is impact.
And impact is not measured by how much you held onto,
but by how much you let go —
and how much of yourself you gave away to make the world
heavier with grace,
lighter with kindness,
richer with love.

In the end, it will not matter what you got.
It will matter what you gave.

That is the true measure of a life.

---

# Chapter 8
# Building Relationships for the Long Haul

## The Fragility of Fast Bonds

Fast bonds feel powerful.
They are fueled by chemistry, by excitement, by the thrill of instant connection.
Two people meet and the world seems to collapse into a single, clear moment of belonging.

But what comes together quickly often comes apart just as fast.

Fast bonds are fragile because they are built on acceleration rather than foundation.
They are forged in intensity, not in endurance.
They mistake immediacy for intimacy.

In the rush of early connection, it is easy to believe that shared excitement will carry a relationship through difficulty.
It is easy to confuse resonance for resilience.

But resonance can be shallow.
It reflects similarity, not strength.

Real relationships — the kind that endure — are not built in the first hours, or even the first months.
They are built slowly, through the invisible accumulation of shared moments:
not only the high points of celebration,
but the low, silent valleys of disappointment, failure, misunderstanding.

The bonds that survive are not the ones that were easiest to form.
They are the ones that were hardest to break.

They are built not on instant agreement, but on the slow negotiation of difference.
Not on the absence of conflict, but on the quiet decision to stay when conflict arises.
Not on the effortless blending of lives, but on the hard work of stitching together two distinct selves without tearing either one apart.

Fast bonds wither when tested because they have not yet been shaped by difficulty.
They have not yet learned the patience required to survive silence, the forgiveness required to survive failure,
the loyalty required to survive distance.

In the early days of a bond, it is easy to promise permanence.
But permanence is not a promise.
It is a practice.

It is practiced not in moments of excitement, but in moments of frustration.
It is practiced when the person you loved for their strengths

reveals their weaknesses.
It is practiced when staying costs more than leaving, and you stay anyway.

The fragility of fast bonds is not a flaw.
It is a feature of time.
Only time can sift connection from infatuation,
trust from attraction,
loyalty from convenience.

To build a relationship for the long haul is to move slowly,
to test quietly,
to allow the bond to deepen not because it is easy,
but because it proves, again and again, that it is stronger than the forces that would tear it apart.

What forms quickly can be beautiful.
But what endures slowly is sacred.

And sacred things are never built in haste.

---

# The Necessity of Forgiveness and Repair

---

No relationship survives without injury.
No bond, however deep or well-intentioned, escapes the inevitable pain of disappointment, misunderstanding, failure.

Where two people meet, they bring their histories.
They bring old wounds and unspoken fears.
They bring habits shaped by a thousand unseen forces.

They bring their imperfect, fragile selves —
and so collision is not a possibility.
It is a certainty.

What separates fragile relationships from lasting ones is not the
absence of harm.
It is the presence of repair.

Forgiveness is not an exception in enduring bonds.
It is a requirement.

Forgiveness is not forgetting.
It is not excusing.
It is not erasing the wrong.

It is the difficult, repeated choice to stay open,
to refuse to let injury harden into resentment,
to hold the wound without turning it into a weapon.

Forgiveness allows a relationship to continue breathing after it
has been hurt.
Without it, even small wounds fester.
Even minor disappointments accumulate, layering into a quiet,
suffocating resentment that eventually fractures what was once
whole.

But forgiveness alone is not enough.

Repair is the work that follows —
the willingness not just to forgive, but to rebuild.
To revisit the point of pain not to assign blame,
but to understand.
To acknowledge the hurt honestly,
to listen carefully,
to offer amends where amends can be made.

Repair is slow.
It cannot be rushed by apology.
It cannot be bypassed by good intentions.
It requires the humility to admit harm,
the patience to rebuild trust grain by grain,
the courage to reopen what would be easier to leave closed.

And repair is costly.
It costs pride.
It costs comfort.
It costs the illusion that we are always right,
always reasonable,
always innocent.

But it is through these costs that depth is gained.

Relationships that endure are not those where injury is avoided,
but those where injury is survived —
where forgiveness is offered not once but many times,
where repair is undertaken not as a single act, but as a way of
living together.

Without forgiveness, there is no future.
Without repair, there is no trust.

Forgiveness keeps the door open.
Repair walks through it.

Together, they form the quiet, invisible architecture of
relationships that last beyond the first failures,
beyond the early ease,
beyond the inevitable pain.

And in the long haul, it is not perfection that sustains a bond.
It is forgiveness.
It is repair.

It is the daily, deliberate choice to begin again.

---

# Why Enduring Relationships Are Built on Imperfection

---

Perfection is seductive.
It promises certainty, control, ease.
It tells us that if we can just find the right person — the flawless
partner, the faultless friend —
then connection will be simple, seamless, unbreakable.

But perfection is a myth.
And those who pursue it in relationships find only
disappointment.
Because people are not machines to be calibrated.
They are not products to be inspected.
They are not blueprints to be executed without error.

They are flawed.
Complicated.
Incomplete.

They are stories in progress,
filled with contradictions, blind spots, unresolved fears.
They are mirrors that sometimes reflect our best selves,
and sometimes reflect what we least want to see.

Real relationships are not built on finding the perfect fit.
They are built on learning to live with imperfection —

both in the other,
and in oneself.

The friendships that endure are not those where nothing ever goes
wrong.
They are those where wrong is acknowledged, absorbed,
forgiven.
Where differences are not eliminated, but respected.
Where flaws are not hidden, but accepted as part of the landscape
—

not barriers to connection, but the texture of it.

The strongest bonds are not those free of disappointment.
They are those where disappointment does not destroy affection.
Where failure does not unravel trust.
Where the recognition of imperfection deepens rather than
diminishes love.

Perfection isolates.
It demands a kind of cleanliness, a kind of sterility, that real life
cannot sustain.

But imperfection invites humility.
It demands patience.
It teaches forgiveness.

It teaches us that loyalty is not the absence of irritation, but the
persistence of care in its presence.
That love is not the absence of flaws, but the decision to hold
someone close despite them.

In a world obsessed with optimization and flawlessness,
it is easy to believe that relationships should be easy,
that struggle is a sign of failure,
that imperfection is a flaw in the design.

But relationships are not products.
They are living things.
And all living things are messy, uneven, marked by growth and decay, by beauty and blemish.

To build a relationship that lasts,
you must make peace with imperfection —
not as a concession,
but as a condition.

You must understand that it is not the absence of flaws that makes someone worth loving.
It is the way they carry their flaws —
the way they remain present despite them,
the way they try, fail, and try again.

And it is the way you remain present with them —
not because they are perfect,
but because they are real.

The real work of building a bond for the long haul is not in demanding perfection.
It is in practicing grace.

Grace for the moments they fall short.
Grace for the ways they are different from you.
Grace for the inevitable mess that any real life contains.

Enduring relationships are not monuments to perfection.
They are monuments to persistence —
to the stubborn, daily choice to love what is imperfect,
and to be loved in return,
just as imperfectly.

# The Quiet Power of Consistency Over Time

Consistency is not glamorous.
It does not dazzle.
It does not announce itself with fireworks or grand declarations.

It is quiet.
It is ordinary.
It is the slow, steady drumbeat beneath the noise of life —
easily overlooked, easily underestimated, but absolutely essential.

In a world drawn to intensity,
where beginnings are celebrated and spectacular moments are
broadcast,
it is easy to forget that what builds anything lasting is not
intensity,
but consistency.

Consistency is showing up.
Not once, not when convenient,
but again and again —
in small, faithful ways that seem unremarkable at the time but
accumulate invisibly.

It is the call returned,
the kindness extended,
the patience offered,
not because it is easy,
but because it has become a practice.

It is the refusal to let distance grow simply because life became busy.
It is the willingness to have the hard conversation instead of letting silence do the slow work of erosion.
It is the decision to forgive,
not once, but as often as necessary.

Consistency does not demand perfection.
It demands presence.
It demands a kind of stubborn loyalty to the bond itself —
a belief that even when emotions waver,
even when circumstances change,
even when doubts whisper,
the act of staying matters.

Over time, consistency builds something that intensity cannot: trust.

Trust is not built in grand gestures.
It is built in the accumulation of small actions repeated faithfully across days,
across seasons,
across years.

It is built in the ordinary moments —
the checking in,
the showing up,
the remembering,
the forgiving.

It is not built by being extraordinary once,
but by being reliably human over and over again.

And as the years pass,
as storms come and go,

as seasons change and life shifts,
it is not the dramatic moments that hold a relationship together.
It is the quiet power of consistency —
the slow, invisible stitching that weaves two lives together,
thread by thread,
until the bond is not a fragile knot,
but a deep, woven fabric that can bear the weight of real life.

Consistency will not always feel exciting.
But it will feel solid.
And in a world where so much is fleeting,
where so much collapses under the pressure of time,
solidity is rare.
It is precious.
It is the mark of something real.

The relationships that endure are not those that burned brightest at
the start.
They are those that, quietly and steadily,
refused to be undone by time.

Consistency does not shout.
It does not sparkle.
It simply stays.

And in staying, it builds what nothing else can:
a love, a trust, a loyalty that lasts.

# Chapter 9
# The High Cost of Reactivity

---

## Why Most People Live Reactively

---

Reactivity feels natural.
It feels immediate, intuitive, alive.
It promises that if you move fast enough, respond quickly
enough, you will stay ahead —
ahead of problems, ahead of competition, ahead of the
disappointments life keeps in reserve.

But what feels natural is not always what is wise.
And what feels urgent is not always what is important.

Most people live reactively not because they lack intelligence,
but because reactivity is rewarded —
by the flashing urgency of the news cycle,
by the dopamine rush of instant response,
by the culture that prizes speed over depth.

Reactivity is easy.
It requires no patience, no strategy, no endurance.

It asks only that you react faster than the next person —
to the email, to the crisis, to the opportunity.

And for a time, reactivity feels powerful.
It feels like momentum.
It feels like progress.

But it is not.

It is motion without direction.
Activity without strategy.
Effort without wisdom.

Reactivity enslaves you to the latest demand, the newest
distraction, the loudest voice.
It traps you in a cycle of endless response,
where your time, your attention, your energy are dictated not by
your goals,
but by whatever is most urgent at any given moment.

In reactivity, there is no reflection.
There is no pause.
There is no space to ask the deeper questions:
What do I want?
Where am I going?
Is this even mine to respond to?

Living reactively means living without intention.
It means surrendering your future to the randomness of the
present.

Because when you are always reacting,
you are never leading.
You are never building.
You are never choosing.

You are simply surviving —
one email, one notification, one crisis at a time.

Most people live this way because it feels safer.
It feels responsible.
It feels like you are doing something.

But reactivity is a kind of sleepwalking.
It moves you, but it does not guide you.

It fills your days with urgency,
but empties your life of meaning.

And by the time you realize it,
you are deep into a life you did not choose,
chasing goals you did not set,
trapped in patterns you did not question.

Reactivity is a silent thief.
It steals not in great, dramatic moments,
but in the slow erosion of your ability to act with clarity and
purpose.

It replaces strategy with panic.
It replaces depth with noise.
It replaces meaning with motion.

Most people live reactively not because they choose it,
but because they have never been taught how costly it really is.

Because the cost of reactivity is not just stress, or distraction, or
exhaustion.

The real cost of reactivity is your life.

# How Reactivity Kills Progress

Progress demands more than movement.
It demands direction.
It demands endurance.
It demands the discipline to pursue what matters long after the
initial excitement fades,
long after the world's attention has shifted elsewhere.

Reactivity, by its nature, destroys this discipline.
It fragments attention.
It scatters energy.
It replaces strategy with urgency, and focus with distraction.

Progress is cumulative.
It builds quietly, invisibly, over time.
Each deliberate action compounds on the last,
each patient choice laying a foundation for the next.

But reactivity interrupts this compounding.
It demands that you abandon your foundation to chase the crisis
of the day,
that you trade the slow work of building for the fast work of
surviving.

When you live reactively, you rarely finish what you start.
You abandon goals not because they have lost their value,
but because something louder, something more urgent, something
shinier has pulled your attention away.

You mistake busyness for productivity.
You mistake exhaustion for accomplishment.
You mistake the churn of constant activity for the quiet, stubborn work that real progress requires.

And so the years pass —
filled with days that were full, but not fulfilling;
busy, but not meaningful;
loud, but not lasting.

The mind trained by reactivity becomes addicted to novelty.
It craves the next thing, the new distraction, the fresh urgency.
It loses the ability to stay with anything long enough to see it through the hard middle,
the unglamorous stretch where most real work happens.

The cost is not just missed opportunities.
It is wasted potential.
It is the erosion of trust —
trust in yourself, trust in your own judgment,
trust in your ability to choose a direction and stay the course.

Because reactivity, repeated often enough, teaches you a dangerous lesson:
that you are at the mercy of events.
That you are powerless to choose your path.
That the best you can do is respond, quickly and endlessly,
to whatever the world throws at you.

But progress belongs to those who resist this lesson.
To those who can sit with discomfort, with boredom, with uncertainty,
and still choose to continue.

To those who can ignore the noise of the moment in service of the larger arc of their own becoming.

Reactivity kills progress not because it stops you from moving, but because it stops you from moving with purpose.

It keeps you spinning when you should be walking.
It keeps you chasing when you should be building.
It keeps you distracted when you should be becoming.

Progress is not fast.
It is not glamorous.
It is not immediate.

It is slow, steady, patient.
It is quiet, deliberate, enduring.

And it is destroyed by the noise of a life lived reactively.

---

## The Emotional Cost — Stress, Burnout, and Regret

---

Reactivity does not just cost you your progress.
It costs you your peace.

A life lived in constant response becomes a life lived in constant tension.
You are always bracing —
for the next demand,
the next disruption,

the next crisis that will pull you away from what matters and drag you into what's merely urgent.

The body does not distinguish between a real emergency and a perceived one.
It reacts the same —
tightening, flooding with stress hormones, preparing for fight or flight.

Reactivity turns this emergency mode into a way of life.
It hardwires anxiety into your days,
teaching your nervous system to expect disruption,
to live on edge,
to treat every notification, every alert, every request as a fire that must be put out immediately.

Over time, this does not just exhaust the body.
It erodes the spirit.

You find yourself always tired,
but never truly at rest.
Always busy,
but never truly productive.
Always moving,
but never truly arriving.

Burnout is not the result of working too hard.
It is the result of working without direction.
Of pouring energy into tasks that do not align with your purpose.
Of responding endlessly without ever choosing carefully.

Reactivity tricks you into believing you have no choice —
that your time, your attention, your energy are not yours to spend deliberately,
but are merely resources to be spent reflexively.

And so you spend them —
on the loudest demands,
the nearest distractions,
the most urgent noise.

At first, it feels manageable.
At first, it feels normal.
Everyone is tired.
Everyone is busy.
Everyone is distracted.

But slowly, imperceptibly, regret begins to accumulate.

Not the regret of a single mistake,
but the slow, quiet regret of years spent chasing what was urgent
instead of what was important.
The regret of waking up to find that while you were busy
responding,
the life you wanted slipped quietly past you.

Stress becomes your baseline.
Burnout becomes your rhythm.
Regret becomes your companion.

Not because you failed to work hard,
but because you failed to work deliberately.

The emotional cost of reactivity is not paid all at once.
It is paid over years,
in the form of opportunities missed,
dreams deferred,
connections neglected,
and a life built on the shifting sands of other people's priorities.

And by the time you notice the cost,
it is not the busyness you will resent.

It is the quiet knowledge that you were busy doing things that did not matter.

Reactivity promises to keep you moving.
But what it really does is keep you from ever arriving.

---

# The Invisibility of Strategic Thinking in a Reactive World

---

Strategic thinking is quiet.
It does not shout.
It does not demand attention.
It does not move in frantic loops of action and reaction.

It waits.
It observes.
It chooses.

In a reactive world, this makes it invisible.
Because what draws attention is speed —
the quick response,
the immediate answer,
the visible hustle.

The strategist does none of these things.
The strategist resists the pull of immediacy.
They are not slower because they are weaker,
but because they understand that not all movement is progress,
and not all noise is signal.

They think in moves, not moments.
They look not just at what is happening now,
but at where now is leading.
They are willing to look foolish in the short term to win in the
long term.

But to a reactive world, this looks like inaction.
It looks like hesitation.
It looks like a lack of urgency.

In cultures addicted to urgency,
patience looks like passivity.
Stillness looks like weakness.
Silence looks like incompetence.

And so the strategist often works unseen —
building not for the next news cycle, but for the next decade.
Choosing not the flashiest opportunity, but the one that
compounds quietly over time.

They are not applauded.
They are not celebrated.
They are often ignored —
until the day comes when the frantic burn out,
the loud collapse,
and the quiet endure.

Strategic thinking requires the discipline to stay invisible when
visibility would cost you your focus.
It requires the strength to prioritize what matters over what
impresses.
It requires the humility to work on timelines that the world does
not understand.

In a reactive world, it is easy to be seduced by immediacy.
It is easy to confuse urgency with importance.
It is easy to believe that the loudest, fastest, busiest are the ones who will win.

But in the long arc,
the quiet builders prevail.
The patient thinkers prevail.
The invisible strategists prevail.

Because while the reactive burn energy chasing the latest crisis,
the strategist conserves energy for the battles that matter.

While the reactive exhaust themselves responding to every signal,
the strategist waits for the signal that matters.

And while the reactive live from noise to noise,
the strategist lives from principle to principle,
from move to move,
from vision to vision.

The world may not notice the strategist at first.
But it will feel their impact in the end.

Because strategy compounds.
It builds.
It endures.

And endurance, not immediacy, is the real currency of a life well lived.

# Chapter 10
# Strategic Thinking Is a Muscle

## Strategic Thinking Is Not a Talent — It's a Discipline

The world likes to treat strategic thinking as a talent —
something you are born with,
something innate, mysterious, untouchable.

But this is a comforting lie.

Strategic thinking is not a talent.
It is not a gift bestowed on a lucky few.
It is a discipline —
trained, built, strengthened through deliberate practice over time.

The strategist is not born seeing further,
or thinking deeper.
They are made —
shaped by the slow, patient work of learning to think differently.

Strategic thinking begins with a choice.
The choice to resist the immediate.

The choice to look past the noise.
The choice to move beyond the urgency of now and to ask the harder questions:
Where is this leading?
What am I really solving for?
What will this decision look like not tomorrow, but ten years from now?

It is a discipline of patience,
a discipline of perspective,
a discipline of humility —
because to think strategically is to admit how little the present moment really reveals.

The strategist trains themselves to zoom out.
To see the pattern beneath the event.
To wait when others rush.
To hold steady when others panic.
To build when others are distracted by the temptation of immediate gains.

And like any discipline, it begins awkwardly.
The first attempts feel unnatural.
The urge to react is strong.
The desire for quick wins, for early applause, for visible movement —
it pulls hard.

But with repetition, the muscle strengthens.

You learn to pause.
You learn to breathe.
You learn to let the first wave of emotion pass without grabbing for action.

You learn to think in terms of systems, not snapshots —
in terms of decades, not days.

Strategic thinking is trained in the moments no one sees —
in the choice to turn down an exciting but misaligned opportunity,
in the decision to invest in a relationship that offers no immediate
advantage,
in the patience to build foundations while others are chasing
facades.

It is not glamorous.
It does not often get immediate rewards.
But it compounds.

And over time, the strategist moves differently.
More quietly.
More slowly.
More surely.

While others chase the appearance of success,
the strategist builds success —
brick by brick, quietly, steadily, inevitably.

Strategic thinking is not a talent.
It is a muscle.
And like all muscles, it strengthens only with use —
only through the repeated discipline of choosing clarity over
noise,
direction over distraction,
patience over panic.

It is not given.
It is earned.
Every day.

# Building Strategic Patience — Thinking in Moves, Not Moments

Impatience is the natural state of the reactive mind.
It demands movement.
It demands results.
It demands to see the immediate effect of every effort,
to cash every investment before it has matured.

But strategic thinking requires a different kind of patience —
a patience that does not wait idly,
but waits actively,
thinking not in moments, but in moves.

Moves are different from moments.
Moments are snapshots —
fleeting, self-contained, isolated from the larger arc of life.
Moments seduce you into reacting —
to the victory, to the setback, to the praise, to the criticism.

But moves are sequences.
They are steps in a larger plan.
They are the deliberate placing of pieces not for immediate payoff,
but for eventual, inevitable positioning.

The strategist builds moves with the patience of someone who
understands that real victories are often invisible for a long time.
They understand that the best moves often look like nothing at

first —
an unnoticed investment in learning,
a quiet relationship nurtured behind the scenes,
a decision to forego a short-term gain that others would chase
without hesitation.

Strategic patience is not passive.
It is not waiting for opportunity to appear.
It is preparing —
stacking the odds, aligning resources, thinking three, four, five
steps ahead.

It is building a position so strong that when the right opportunity
does appear,
you are ready not just to react,
but to move decisively, with force and clarity.

This patience is hard to practice in a culture that glorifies the
moment —
that celebrates overnight success, viral fame, quick victories.

But most of what looks sudden from the outside is the product of
years of invisible preparation.
The visible breakthrough is only the final move in a long, quiet
game of positioning.

Strategic patience means accepting that not every action will yield
immediate results.
It means knowing that many of your best moves will look, for a
time, like mistakes —
too slow, too cautious, too quiet for a world obsessed with noise.

It means trusting in the compound effect of deliberate, aligned
effort over years,
while others exhaust themselves chasing after weeks.

It is the patience of the chess master,
not the impatience of the gambler.
It is the patience of the builder,
not the impatience of the opportunist.

Thinking in moves, not moments,
is what separates those who achieve fleeting wins from those who
build enduring legacies.

Because anyone can succeed once by accident.
But to succeed repeatedly,
to endure across cycles and storms and seasons —
that requires more than luck.
It requires a mind trained not to chase moments,
but to build moves.

---

## Training Foresight — Seeing Beyond Immediate Outcomes

---

Foresight is not prophecy.
It is not the ability to predict the future with precision.
It is the ability to think in longer arcs —
to see how today's decisions echo into tomorrow's realities.

Most people are trained to think in immediate outcomes.
Did this work?
Did it fail?

What did I get?
What did I lose?

Their vision stops at the next result,
the next reaction,
the next reward or setback.

But the strategist knows that immediate outcomes are only
ripples.
They are not the tide.
They are not the current.

They are noise.

Training foresight requires the discipline to look past these ripples
—

to ask not just what will happen next,
but what this move sets in motion,
what doors it opens,
what costs it hides.

It requires the willingness to delay judgment —
to resist the urge to label every result a success or failure before
its consequences have unfolded.

Foresight means understanding that most outcomes cannot be
evaluated at the point of impact.
They must be judged by how they compound over time —
by what they lead to three steps down the road,
not by what they deliver in the next five minutes.

It means thinking not just about whether an opportunity is good,
but whether it aligns with the larger shape of the life you are
building.
Not just whether a win feels satisfying now,
but whether it strengthens or weakens your position later.

It is asking:
If I take this shortcut now, what long path am I closing off later?
If I say yes to this easy gain, what harder, deeper growth am I
sacrificing?

Foresight is not just about seeing threats on the horizon.
It is about understanding how your present choices create your
future constraints —
how today's compromise becomes tomorrow's trap,
how today's discipline becomes tomorrow's freedom.

The strategist trains foresight slowly.
By studying history —
not the headlines, but the patterns.
By studying failures —
not the moments of collapse, but the years of drift that preceded
them.
By studying success —
not the celebrations, but the unseen years of preparation that made
them possible.

And by studying themselves —
their tendencies, their habits, their blind spots —
learning how their own impulsive reactions create cycles that
must be broken if a different future is to be built.

Training foresight is a lonely discipline.
Few will encourage you to think this way.
Most will push you to act, to react, to seize the nearest prize.

But foresight is not concerned with prizes.
It is concerned with positioning —
with being in the right place not just once,
but repeatedly,

sustainably,
durably.

It is the difference between those who win once
and those who endure.

Because in the end,
it is not the person who moves first who wins.
It is the person who moves best —
with foresight,
with patience,
with clarity of purpose stretching far beyond the noise of now.

---

## The Difference Between Planning and Strategic Thinking

---

Planning feels safe.
It feels responsible.
It feels like control.

You make a list.
You set a timeline.
You plot the steps from here to there.

Planning offers the illusion that if you can just get the sequence right,
the outcome will take care of itself.

But planning is not strategy.
And mistaking the two is one of the most costly errors a person can make.

Plans assume stability.
They assume that the world will cooperate,
that conditions will remain constant,
that what works today will work tomorrow.

But the world is not stable.
It moves.
It shifts.
It breaks patterns without warning.

A plan is a script.
And the moment reality refuses to follow the script,
the planner freezes.

Strategic thinking is different.

Strategic thinking does not begin with a script.
It begins with a principle:
The world will change.
People will change.
Conditions will change.

Strategic thinking is not about predicting the future.
It is about preparing to adapt to it.
It is about building a position strong enough to survive uncertainty,
flexible enough to respond to the unexpected,
focused enough to stay aligned even when the path twists.

The planner asks:
What steps must I follow?

The strategist asks:

What game am I really playing?

What position do I need to build that will survive more than one outcome?

Planning focuses on tactics —
the specific moves to get from point A to point B.

Strategic thinking focuses on positioning —
building strength, resilience, leverage,
so that no matter what happens between A and B,
you can adapt and prevail.

Plans are fragile.
They are brittle against the chaos of real life.

Strategy is fluid.
It moves with conditions.
It bends without breaking.
It shifts without losing sight of the ultimate goal.

Strategic thinkers do not abandon planning altogether.
But they hold their plans lightly.
They treat them as tools, not as laws.
They understand that the map is not the territory,
and that success belongs not to those with the perfect plan,
but to those with the flexible mind.

In a world obsessed with certainty,
planning feels comforting.
It gives the illusion of mastery.

But real mastery belongs to those who can navigate uncertainty,
who can make decisions not just based on the next step,
but on the larger game they are playing.

Strategic thinking is not rigid.
It is not formulaic.
It is not chained to a script.

It is alive.
It is responsive.
It is enduring.

And in a world that punishes rigidity and rewards adaptability,
it is not the planner who endures,
but the strategist.

Because the strategist knows:
The map will change.
The path will shift.
The ground will move.

But if you are thinking strategically,
you can move with it.
You can move through it.

And you can still arrive.

---

# Chapter 11
# Tools and Frameworks for Strategic Living

---

## Mental Models — Thinking in Principles, Not Reactions

---

A mind without structure is a mind at the mercy of its impulses.
It reacts.
It drifts.
It seizes on whatever feels urgent, mistaking instinct for insight.

But strategic living requires more than instinct.
It requires a deeper architecture —
a set of frameworks that anchor your thinking,
that slow the rush of reaction,
that guide you when the surface of life becomes too noisy to trust.

Mental models are these frameworks.
They are the patterns beneath patterns.
The principles beneath decisions.

The quiet scaffolding that supports clear thought when the easy path is confusion.

A mental model is not a trick.
It is not a shortcut to avoid thinking.
It is the opposite:
a disciplined way of forcing yourself to think better,
to see beyond the obvious,
to resist the pull of the first, easiest answer.

Mental models invite you to ask different questions.
Instead of reacting, you step back and ask:
What kind of problem is this?
What is the real lever here?
Am I seeing the full picture, or only what is immediately visible?

They teach you to think not in isolated decisions,
but in systems.
Not in moments,
but in consequences.
Not in appearances,
but in underlying structures.

The strategist does not rely on inspiration.
They rely on models —
on ways of seeing that sharpen judgment,
that reveal the hidden mechanics beneath surface chaos.

Mental models slow you down —
not to paralyze you,
but to prevent you from moving blindly.

They ask you to consider opportunity cost:
If I say yes to this, what am I saying no to?
They ask you to consider second-order consequences:

If I do this now, what happens next — and after that?
They ask you to consider inversions:
Instead of asking how to succeed, what would guarantee failure
— and how can I avoid it?

They demand humility.
Because models, when properly used, reveal not only what you know,
but what you don't.
They show the gaps in your understanding,
the weak points in your assumptions,
the biases you are tempted to indulge.

They do not make decision-making easy.
They make it serious.

Mental models are not crutches for the lazy thinker.
They are weights for the strong thinker —
tools that, when lifted properly, build the strength of judgment,
the endurance of patience,
the clarity of long-term vision.

And in a world addicted to surface thinking,
they are rare.
They are powerful.
They are what separate the strategist from the reactive,
the builder from the drifter,
the enduring from the transient.

To live strategically is to collect models,
to sharpen them,
to return to them again and again —
not as answers,
but as disciplines.

Because it is not the answers you carry that determine your future.
It is the quality of the questions you know how to ask.

And mental models —
at their best —
teach you how to ask better questions.

---

## Scenario Planning — Preparing for Multiple Futures

---

Most people prepare for the future as if there is only one.
They imagine a straight line —
a single, inevitable unfolding where today's trends continue uninterrupted,
where tomorrow is merely an extension of today.

But the strategist knows better.

The strategist knows that the future is not a line.
It is a branching tree —
an expanding web of possibilities, uncertainties, collisions, and surprises.
No single path is guaranteed.
No outcome is certain.

Scenario planning is the discipline of preparing not for one future, but for many.

It is the refusal to anchor yourself to a single prediction.
It is the humility to accept that the future is not something you control,
but something you must navigate.

Scenario planning begins with imagination —
the structured, disciplined imagination of what could happen if the trends bend,
if the ground shifts,
if the unthinkable becomes real.

It asks:
If the economy collapses, what will I wish I had prepared?
If technology changes faster than expected, how will I adapt?
If this partnership fails, what is my next move?
If this industry dies, what else have I built that can survive?

But it is not fear-mongering.
It is not pessimism.
It is preparation —
preparation for volatility,
preparation for surprise,
preparation for resilience in the face of futures no one else saw coming.

Scenario planning trains the mind to stay loose,
to avoid overcommitting to a single narrative.
It teaches you to build strategies that are robust —
not because they bet on being right,
but because they can survive being wrong.

It shifts the goal from prediction to adaptability.
It moves you from rigid plans to flexible positioning.

The strategist does not cling to one vision of the future.
They prepare for a range of outcomes,
positioning themselves not for perfection,
but for resilience.

They understand that success belongs not to those who guess
correctly once,
but to those who survive the widest range of possibilities.

Scenario planning forces you to think in contingencies.
It sharpens your ability to recognize when the world is shifting,
when the assumptions you once trusted no longer hold,
when it is time not to react blindly,
but to pivot intelligently.

It keeps you from being paralyzed by surprise,
because surprise was always part of the model.

It keeps you from being broken by change,
because change was always part of the preparation.

The future will not conform to your plans.
But it will reward your readiness.

Scenario planning is not a guarantee against failure.
It is a hedge against fragility.
It is a commitment to staying flexible,
staying thoughtful,
staying prepared.

Because in a world that no longer rewards certainty,
the real strategic advantage is not in knowing what will happen —
but in being ready for whatever does.

# The Power of Pre-Mortems — Learning to Fail in Advance

Most people wait for failure to teach them.
They move forward blindly,
believing in the momentum of their plans,
trusting that effort will be enough,
hoping that good intentions will shield them from collapse.

And when failure comes — as it often does —
they are caught unprepared,
scrambling to make sense of what went wrong,
rushing to recover what might have been protected.

The strategist moves differently.

The strategist practices failure in advance.

This is the discipline of the pre-mortem —
the deliberate act of imagining the collapse before it happens,
of tracing the hidden vulnerabilities while there is still time to act,
of asking the hard questions while success is still within reach.

A pre-mortem is not pessimism.
It is preparation.

It does not begin with the question,
*How will we succeed?*
It begins with the harder question,
*How could this fail?*

What assumptions are we making that could collapse under pressure?
What blind spots are we ignoring because they are inconvenient to see?
What hidden risks are we underestimating because they do not fit the story we want to tell?

The pre-mortem demands brutal honesty —
not just with the external world,
but with yourself.

It requires the courage to admit that effort is not enough,
that good intentions are not guarantees,
that no plan, no matter how elegant, is immune to the rough edges of reality.

By forcing yourself to walk the path of failure before it happens,
you uncover the weak points —
the brittle assumptions,
the neglected contingencies,
the vulnerabilities that would otherwise remain hidden until it is too late.

And once uncovered,
you can reinforce them.
You can build flexibility where there was fragility.
You can create contingencies where there was complacency.
You can design a path not just to success,
but through failure —
so that even if the worst happens,
you are prepared to bend, not break.

The pre-mortem is not an act of fear.
It is an act of respect —

respect for reality,
respect for complexity,
respect for the fact that the world owes you no favors,
and that resilience is built not on optimism alone,
but on preparation.

Most people experience failure as a surprise.
The strategist experiences it as a possibility already studied,
already understood,
already planned for.

Because they know:
Failure is not the enemy.
Unpreparedness is.

And the best way to survive the future
is to practice failing in advance —
quietly, seriously, invisibly —
until failure loses its power to destroy,
and becomes only another move in the larger game of endurance.

---

# Living Strategically — Moving from Tactics to Vision

---

Tactics are seductive.
They are close at hand.
They offer the satisfaction of quick wins,

the illusion of progress,
the comfort of movement.

A clever tactic can win a battle.
But it cannot win a war.

A well-executed tactic can solve a problem.
But it cannot build a life.

Living strategically requires a shift —
from tactics to vision.
From the immediate to the enduring.
From winning moments to shaping trajectories.

Tactics ask:
What can I do today to gain an advantage?
Vision asks:
What kind of life am I building,
and how must I act today to stay faithful to that life?

Tactics are about action.
Vision is about direction.

Without vision, tactics become frantic —
a scatter of effort across too many fronts,
a thousand short sprints without a finish line.

Vision does not reject tactics.
It organizes them.
It subordinates them to something larger.
It disciplines action with purpose.

Vision is not a dream.
It is not a vague hope for someday.
It is a structure —

a coherent sense of what you are moving toward,
and why it matters.

Vision slows you down when the world tries to rush you.
It holds you steady when failure tempts you to abandon the path.
It clarifies decisions when every option seems equally urgent.

Without vision, life becomes a series of reactions —
to opportunities, to crises, to other people's expectations.

With vision, life becomes a series of moves —
intentional, patient, cumulative.

Vision demands sacrifice.
You cannot chase every opportunity and stay faithful to a single direction.
You cannot please everyone and still build the life you are meant to build.
You cannot have it all, all the time, without losing what matters most.

But vision also grants freedom —
the freedom to say no without guilt,
the freedom to wait without anxiety,
the freedom to build without needing immediate applause.

Living strategically means choosing vision over tactics —
choosing the slow accumulation of something meaningful
over the fast consumption of things that merely distract.

It means accepting that real progress is measured not in how much you can do today,
but in how well today's actions align with the life you are committed to creating.

It means trading the illusion of busy success
for the quieter, deeper success of staying on course
when others have forgotten where they were going.

Vision is the compass.
Tactics are the steps.
Strategy is the art of aligning the two —
day after day,
decision after decision,
until what you have built is not merely a list of accomplishments,
but a life that holds together —
coherent, enduring, true.

---

# Chapter 12
# The Myth of Overnight Success

---

## The Invisible Years — What the World Doesn't See

---

Success loves a story.
It loves the neat arc, the rapid rise, the sudden breakthrough.
It loves the myth of the overnight success —
the idea that greatness arrives all at once,
wrapped in glamour,
free of mess,
untainted by the slow grind of ordinary work.

But every real success story hides the same truth:
before the moment everyone sees,
there are years no one notices.

Years of quiet labor.
Years of obscurity.
Years of effort that looked, to the outside world, like failure —
or worse, like nothing at all.

The novelist who "burst onto the scene" with a bestseller
spent a decade writing manuscripts no one read.
The entrepreneur who "came out of nowhere"
spent years building companies that collapsed quietly in the
background.
The athlete who "became an overnight sensation"
spent lonely mornings training when no one was watching,
when no one cared.

The world sees the moment of arrival.
It does not see the years of invisible departure —
the long, slow pulling away from mediocrity,
the painful separation from comfort,
the gradual ascent through discipline, repetition, failure.

It does not see the sacrifices that had no immediate reward.
It does not see the patience that was mocked as passivity.
It does not see the resilience that was mistaken for stubbornness.

It sees only the final scene,
not the endless rehearsals.

The myth of overnight success is comforting
because it suggests that success is a lightning strike —
a matter of timing, of luck, of magic.

But the reality is harder.
The reality is that success is built incrementally —
hour by hour,
day by day,
decision by decision —
in spaces so small, so ordinary,
that they escape the attention of a world addicted to spectacle.

The invisible years are not a detour.
They are the path.

They are the place where craft is refined,
where character is shaped,
where the quiet, unglamorous foundation is laid
for what will someday look, to the outsider,
like sudden brilliance.

But brilliance is never sudden.
It is patient.
It is cumulative.
It is built in silence.

The world will never celebrate your invisible years.
It will never applaud your unnoticed mornings,
your unrewarded persistence,
your private failures.

But those years will shape you more than any moment of fame
ever could.
They will teach you the kind of resilience that endures beyond
applause,
the kind of discipline that survives beyond trends,
the kind of quiet excellence that does not depend on recognition
to matter.

The myth of overnight success is a lie.
But the truth is better:
Success is a long obedience in the same direction.
It is slow, it is unseen, it is uncelebrated —
and it is, for those who endure, unstoppable.

# Why the World Celebrates the Arrival, Not the Journey

The world loves the arrival.
It loves the moment the doors swing open and someone steps into the light —
polished, finished, victorious.

It loves the debut, the headline, the award, the announcement.
The final product, clean and dazzling,
stripped of the long, complicated history that made it possible.

The world does not love the journey.
It does not love the quiet years of obscurity,
the failures that leave no impressive scars,
the private battles that will never be recounted in neat soundbites.

It does not love the loneliness of effort without audience,
the patience of building without applause,
the faith required to persist without guarantees.

The journey is messy.
It resists easy storytelling.
It does not fit into the neat narratives that society demands —
stories of rapid ascent, of genius discovered, of fortune stumbled upon.

The journey is slow.
It is filled with detours, wrong turns, invisible progress.

It asks for years of loyalty to a process that shows no immediate reward.

And so the world edits it out.
It celebrates the arrival because the arrival is simple.
It is clear.
It is visible.

It reduces a complex becoming to a single moment of being —
as if everything before that moment was irrelevant,
as if the arrival happened by chance or fate or destiny.

But the arrival is not the miracle.
The journey is.

The miracle is not that someone succeeded.
It is that they endured —
through failure, through doubt, through obscurity.

It is that they remained loyal to a vision when no one else could see it.
It is that they built slowly, patiently, invisibly,
when the world demanded speed and spectacle.

The world celebrates the arrival because it is easy to understand.
But you must remember:
The arrival is only a flash.
It is a single frame in a long, difficult film.

If you build your life chasing arrivals,
you will be chasing shadows —
hollow moments that fade as quickly as they come.

But if you build your life embracing the journey,
honoring the slow, invisible accumulation of effort,
valuing the process more than the product,

you will have something the world cannot give —
and cannot take away.

You will have depth.
You will have resilience.
You will have the quiet pride of someone who did not just arrive,
but became.

The world will celebrate your arrival.
But you must learn to celebrate your journey —
because it is the journey that will sustain you long after the
applause fades.

---

## The Danger of Believing in Sudden Transformation

---

Sudden transformation is a seductive idea.
It suggests that change can happen in an instant —
that one insight, one event, one breakthrough can remake a life
overnight.

It flatters us with the promise that hard work can be bypassed,
that time can be cheated,
that discipline can be replaced by discovery.

But sudden transformation is a myth.
And believing in it is dangerous.

It leads to impatience.
It leads to despair.
It leads to the false conviction that if change does not come quickly,
it will not come at all.

It teaches us to chase moments instead of building movements.
It tempts us to abandon slow progress for the illusion of rapid revolution.
It encourages us to quit too soon,
to declare defeat when the breakthrough doesn't arrive on schedule.

Real transformation is not sudden.
It is slow.
It is cumulative.
It is built in layers so thin they are invisible —
moments of effort,
moments of failure,
moments of resilience,
stacked one atop the other until,
without noticing,
you have become someone new.

Transformation is not a single event.
It is a process —
a series of small, deliberate choices repeated in obscurity long enough to create a shift that feels sudden only in retrospect.

The danger of believing in sudden transformation is that it blinds you to the power of steady effort.
It devalues the long, slow work of becoming.
It teaches you to dismiss the small gains,

to overlook the daily disciplines,
to abandon the journey when the milestones seem too far apart.

But the truth is simple and unforgiving:
Those who endure the small disciplines are the ones who
eventually experience the large breakthroughs.

Not because they found a shortcut.
Not because they stumbled onto a secret.
But because they stayed when others left.
Because they worked when others waited.
Because they believed in process when others demanded
miracles.

Transformation is not magic.
It is a slow unfolding.
It is the result of fidelity to a vision through seasons of
invisibility,
through years of work that feels, to the outside world, like nothing
at all.

It is the quiet revolution that happens inside —
in the way you think,
the way you choose,
the way you stay loyal to the hard thing long enough to make it
yours.

Sudden transformation is a comforting myth.
But real transformation belongs to those willing to live without
the comfort of myth —
to those willing to trade the fantasy of the breakthrough
for the hard, slow beauty of the becoming.

# The True Pace of Mastery and Long-Term Success

Mastery moves at a different pace than the world expects.
It is not hurried.
It is not frantic.
It does not yield to the demands of impatience.

Mastery moves slowly —
almost invisibly —
growing like roots beneath the surface,
strengthening in silence long before it becomes visible to the
outside world.

The true pace of mastery is deliberate.
It is measured in years, not weeks.
It is built not through bursts of inspiration,
but through the slow, steady accumulation of discipline.

Mastery demands repetition.
The kind of repetition that feels dull at times,
the kind that tests your patience,
the kind that forces you to confront the limits of your own
endurance.

It demands humility —
the willingness to remain a beginner longer than feels
comfortable,

the willingness to fail quietly,
the willingness to improve by margins too small to notice in the moment.

It demands resilience —
the ability to keep working when progress feels invisible,
the ability to endure the seasons when no one notices,
the ability to trust that what you are building in obscurity will one day stand in the light.

Long-term success follows the same quiet rhythm.
It is not a sprint.
It is not a leap.
It is a series of patient steps taken day after day,
without applause,
without shortcuts,
without certainty.

The true pace of mastery and long-term success is too slow to satisfy the hunger for immediate results.
But it is steady enough to outlast the noise.
It is consistent enough to build something real.
It is persistent enough to carry you past the point where most people quit.

Those who understand this pace do not rush.
They do not panic when results are slow.
They do not abandon their craft because it has not yet yielded visible rewards.

They stay.

They work.

They trust the slow accumulation of effort,
the silent compounding of practice,
the invisible strengthening of character.

And in time —
not overnight, not suddenly, not by accident —
they arrive.

But by the time they arrive,
they have become something different.
Something that was not built in a moment,
but shaped by years of quiet labor.

The world will call it talent.
It will call it luck.
It will call it genius.

But you will know better.

You will know it was patience.
You will know it was persistence.
You will know it was a long obedience in the same direction,
a loyalty to the slow, invisible pace of real becoming.

The true pace of mastery is not for the impatient.
But it is for the enduring.
And in a world chasing fast success,
endurance is the greatest advantage you can have.

---

# Chapter 13
# Building a Long-Term Mindset

## The Shift from Immediate Rewards to Lasting Value

The mind trained by modern life is addicted to immediacy.
It expects quick rewards.
It craves fast feedback.
It is built to prefer the visible, the instant, the gratifying.

Everything in the world reinforces this addiction —
the instant notification,
the immediate applause,
the rapid gratification of shallow accomplishment.

But a long-term life cannot be built on the foundations of immediacy.
It requires a different kind of mind —
a mind trained to resist the hunger for instant reward,
to look beyond the next milestone,
to think not in days or months, but in decades.

Building a long-term mindset begins with a shift —
a shift from asking, *What do I get now?*
to asking, *What will endure?*

It is the shift from chasing attention
to cultivating depth.
From seeking applause
to building resilience.
From maximizing the moment
to investing in what outlasts the moment.

The long-term mind knows that most rewards worth having do
not arrive quickly.
They are slow to form,
quiet in their arrival,
invisible in their early stages.

Trust is slow.
Reputation is slow.
Wisdom is slow.

And so the long-term mind adjusts its expectations.
It trades the sugar rush of early validation
for the slow nourishment of lasting value.

It is not that it abandons achievement.
It is that it redefines achievement.
It seeks not the flash of recognition,
but the quiet satisfaction of craft honed over time,
of relationships strengthened through trials,
of character shaped by years of invisible choices.

This shift is not natural.
It must be practiced.
It must be reinforced against the noise of a world that will always

push you toward the easy win,
the fast return,
the cheap satisfaction.

The long-term mind becomes comfortable with delayed
gratification.
It understands that the things that grow slowly
grow deeply.

It understands that the structures that last
are built not on urgency,
but on patience.

It understands that the lives we admire most
were not assembled quickly,
but constructed carefully —
over years of quiet labor,
over decades of unseen faithfulness.

To build a long-term mindset is to build an inner architecture
strong enough to resist the tides of impatience,
stubborn enough to withstand the storms of discouragement,
loyal enough to endure the slow, invisible years.

It is a shift from speed to durability,
from momentary gains to permanent growth,
from the fleeting to the foundational.

And in a world chasing faster and faster rewards,
the long-term mind becomes not only rare —
it becomes invincible.

# Why Playing the Long Game Changes Your Priorities

When you commit to the long game,
your priorities shift —
sometimes slowly, sometimes all at once,
but always profoundly.

The things that once seemed urgent lose their pull.
The temptations that once seemed irresistible begin to look small.
The distractions that once demanded your attention fade into
background noise.

Because the long game recalibrates your sense of what matters.

In the short game, you prioritize appearances —
how things look now,
how quickly you can prove yourself,
how immediately you can be rewarded.

In the long game, you prioritize substance —
how things will endure,
how deeply they are built,
how aligned they are with the person you are becoming.

In the short game, success is defined by proximity —
How fast can I get there?
How close am I to the next win?

In the long game, success is defined by trajectory —
Am I moving in the right direction,
even if the arrival is still years away?

The long game shifts your priorities from speed to endurance,
from visibility to authenticity,
from quick wins to deep roots.

You begin to value relationships not for what they can offer today,
but for what they can withstand over time.
You begin to value work not for how impressive it looks from a
distance,
but for how meaningful it feels from the inside.

You begin to measure progress not in headlines or metrics,
but in the quiet accumulation of trust, skill, character.

The long game teaches you to be suspicious of shortcuts —
to question anything that promises everything without cost,
to recognize that what is easily gained is often easily lost.

It teaches you to say no more often —
no to opportunities that do not align with your deeper purpose,
no to distractions that pull you away from your real work,
no to the shallow validation that feels good today but weakens
you tomorrow.

The long game forces you to confront the reality of trade-offs.
You cannot have everything.
You cannot do everything.
You must choose.

And in choosing, you must be willing to let go of the good
to stay faithful to the great.
You must be willing to endure seasons where the rewards are not
visible,

where the fruits of your labor are still underground,
where the world cannot yet see what you are building —
but you can.

Playing the long game does not make life easier.
It makes life clearer.

It demands sacrifices —
of speed, of comfort, of applause.

But it offers something far greater in return —
a life aligned with something larger than urgency,
a life built on principles rather than reactions,
a life moving not just forward,
but upward —
slowly, steadily, invisibly —
until what you have built cannot be undone by time or tide.

---

## Training Endurance — Building Mental and Emotional Stamina

---

Endurance is not a natural gift.
It is not a trait that some possess and others lack.
It is a discipline —
one that must be trained slowly, deliberately, relentlessly.

In the short game, stamina is not required.
You sprint.
You push hard for a moment.

You burn brightly and briefly.
Then you stop.

But the long game demands a different kind of strength —
not the strength to surge,
but the strength to persist.

It demands the ability to continue long after the novelty has worn off,
long after the initial excitement has faded,
long after the world has moved on to the next shiny thing.

Endurance is the quiet power to keep showing up,
to keep doing the unglamorous work,
to keep investing in something that may not reward you for years.

Mental endurance is the ability to stay focused when distractions clamor for your attention,
to resist the urge to chase the next quick win,
to hold fast to your direction even when the path is unclear.

It is the discipline to think beyond the next deadline,
to plan beyond the next season,
to dream beyond the next applause.

Emotional endurance is the capacity to withstand disappointment without collapse,
to absorb failure without losing faith,
to remain patient when progress is slow and recognition is absent.

It is the resilience to keep believing in the unseen work,
to keep trusting the process when outcomes are uncertain,
to keep your heart steady when the world tries to shake it.

Endurance is not built in dramatic moments.
It is built in the quiet repetition of ordinary days —

in the mornings you show up to work without inspiration,
in the afternoons you continue despite discouragement,
in the evenings you recommit to the path without needing proof
that it's working.

It is built in choosing persistence over perfection,
discipline over distraction,
patience over panic.

Training endurance means learning to carry weight without
visible reward.
It means learning to love the process more than the outcome.
It means understanding that slow progress is still progress,
and that delayed gratification is not denial,
but preparation for something deeper,
something more lasting.

Endurance is not a sprint.
It is not a burst of energy.

It is a quiet loyalty to your highest values,
sustained through seasons of drought and flood alike.

It is what separates those who merely start
from those who finish.
It is what separates those who wish for success
from those who become it —
not once,
but again and again,
across the long, unfolding landscape of a life built not for speed,
but for substance.

# The Quiet Power of Staying the Course

There is a power in staying the course that the world rarely
celebrates.
It is not dramatic.
It does not flash or roar.
It does not announce itself with grand gestures.

It is quiet.
It is steady.
It is almost invisible —
until it is not.

Most people quit before they ever encounter this power.
They change directions at the first sign of resistance,
pivot at the first feeling of discomfort,
abandon their path when the excitement fades and the grind
begins.

They mistake boredom for failure.
They mistake delay for defeat.
They mistake the slow unfolding of something lasting
for the absence of progress.

But those who stay the course know better.

They know that greatness is not built in the burst of a moment,
but in the persistence of many small, patient moments stacked
atop each other.

They know that the work that matters most is the work that demands not just energy,
but endurance.

The power of staying the course is not in blind stubbornness.
It is not in refusing to adapt or learn or evolve.
It is in remaining loyal to the deeper direction,
even as the terrain shifts.

It is in resisting the seduction of the shortcut.
It is in ignoring the noise of temporary trends.
It is in trusting that what is being built slowly is being built strongly.

Staying the course is an act of faith —
faith not in the immediate,
but in the eventual.
Faith not in the ease of the journey,
but in the worth of the destination.

It is the courage to be consistent when consistency is neither praised nor rewarded.
It is the patience to keep planting seeds when the harvest is still invisible.
It is the discipline to keep moving forward when the applause has faded,
and the only voice urging you onward is your own.

The world will tell you to pivot, to change, to chase what is trending.
It will tell you that endurance is outdated,
that loyalty to a long vision is naïve.

But look closely —
and you will see that the most remarkable lives,

the most enduring legacies,
the most profound successes,
belong not to those who moved fastest,
but to those who stayed the course longest.

Staying the course is not passive.
It is not resignation.

It is an active loyalty to the best version of your future —
the version that cannot be rushed,
that cannot be hacked,
that cannot be built on anything less than slow, patient, daily
commitment.

The quiet power of staying the course is that it builds what time
cannot erode.
It creates strength that applause cannot inflate,
and disappointment cannot deflate.

It is not the loudest power.
But it is the deepest.

And in the end, it is the only power that truly lasts.

---

# Chapter 14
# What You Must Give Up to Go Long

## The Illusion of Control Over Timing

One of the first illusions you must surrender
if you want to go long
is the illusion of control over timing.

We are taught to believe in timelines —
that effort leads to predictable rewards,
that success arrives on schedule,
that life will unfold neatly if we simply plan well and work hard
enough.

But the truth is harsher — and freer.

You can control your effort.
You can control your discipline.
You can control your commitment to the craft,
to the work,
to the vision you are building.

But you cannot control the timing.

You cannot control when the breakthrough comes —
or if it comes in the form you expect.

You cannot control when the market shifts,
when the world pays attention,
when the opportunity you've been preparing for finally opens.

You cannot force recognition.
You cannot hurry mastery.
You cannot compress the seasons of becoming into a schedule
that fits your impatience.

Going long demands that you give up this illusion.
It demands that you plant without knowing when the harvest will come,
that you build without knowing when the world will notice,
that you stay loyal to the invisible process
without demanding that it reveal its fruits on your timeline.

It demands the surrender of control
not as a weakness,
but as a wisdom —
a deep acceptance that some things grow in their own time,
regardless of your effort,
your intelligence,
your will.

This surrender is not passive.
It is not giving up.
It is not quitting.

It is the active choice to keep showing up,
to keep preparing,

to keep believing —
without the false comfort of deadlines.

It is a loyalty to the process,
not the payoff.
It is a devotion to the work,
not the reward.

The illusion of control over timing will tempt you to quit too soon.
It will whisper that if success hasn't arrived by now,
it is proof that it never will.

But the reality is simpler, and harder:
Some of the most important work happens beneath the surface,
unseen and uncelebrated,
until it is ready —
not on your clock,
but on its own.

To go long is to trade the comfort of control
for the discomfort of patience.

It is to trust that time is not your enemy,
but your silent ally —
working in the background,
compounding your efforts in ways you cannot yet see.

It is to understand that you are not on a schedule.
You are on a path.
And the path, if you stay on it,
leads not just to a destination,
but to a transformation.

# The Addiction to Validation and Why You Must Resist It

Validation is intoxicating.
It offers immediate proof that you are seen,
that you are valued,
that you are moving in the right direction.

It arrives in applause, in recognition,
in the quick currency of likes and praise.
It soothes the doubt, quiets the fear,
fills the gaps where patience and resilience are still being formed.

But validation is a dangerous drug.
It feels like fuel,
but it is a trap.

Because once you begin to depend on it,
your loyalty shifts —
from the work to the response,
from the process to the approval,
from the long game to the short reward.

You begin to optimize for attention instead of endurance.
You begin to chase what is popular instead of what is true.
You begin to serve the expectations of others
instead of the vision that once called you into the difficult, private
labor of building something that matters.

Validation is addictive precisely because it feels harmless.
It feels like confirmation.
It feels like progress.

But slowly, quietly, it erodes the independence of mind and the loyalty to craft
that long-term success demands.

To go long, you must resist the addiction to validation.
You must learn to do the work without applause.
You must learn to measure your progress by internal standards,
not external reactions.

You must develop the discipline to continue when the world is silent,
when the work feels invisible,
when no one is watching —
especially then.

You must understand that validation is not a signal of value.
It is a signal of attention.
And attention is fickle, shallow, fleeting.

The work that endures —
the work that matters —
is rarely validated early.
It is often misunderstood, ignored, doubted.

Because true value is not built for quick approval.
It is built for deep impact.

The addiction to validation will tempt you to move faster,
to take shortcuts,
to abandon the slow, quiet process that real mastery demands.

It will tempt you to turn away from the deep work
toward the shiny reward.

But to go long is to stay loyal to the invisible standards.
To the standard of consistency when no one is clapping.
To the standard of quality when no one is noticing.
To the standard of integrity when no one is rewarding it.

It is to trust that real validation —
the kind that matters —
comes not from the crowd,
but from the quiet knowledge that you stayed the course
when it would have been easier to seek attention instead.

To go long is to break the addiction to validation.
And in breaking it,
to gain something better:
the freedom to work deeply,
to build patiently,
to endure quietly.

Until the work speaks for itself —
whether or not the world is listening.

---

# Letting Go of the Need for Speed

---

Speed is seductive.
It flatters your ambition.

It promises quick results, instant gratification, the illusion of control.

It whispers that if you just move fast enough,
you can bypass the slow, painful parts of growth —
the uncertainty,
the patience,
the repetition without reward.

In a world obsessed with acceleration,
speed is often mistaken for progress.
Busy schedules are mistaken for productive lives.
Quick wins are mistaken for lasting victories.

But speed, unchecked, is a form of drift.
It pulls you forward without asking whether you are moving in
the right direction.
It fills your days with motion,
but empties them of meaning.

When you live by the need for speed,
you become reactive rather than strategic.
You chase what is urgent rather than what is important.
You trade the deep work of building something enduring
for the shallow work of keeping up.

The need for speed sacrifices depth for momentum,
quality for quantity,
wisdom for immediacy.

And worst of all,
it blinds you to the truth that anything truly worth having —
anything truly worth becoming —
cannot be rushed.

Mastery cannot be rushed.
Trust cannot be rushed.
Character cannot be rushed.
Wisdom cannot be rushed.

The foundations that hold up a meaningful life
are laid slowly,
carefully,
out of sight.

They are built through quiet, repeated effort,
through patience in seasons of invisibility,
through discipline when the rewards are too distant to see.

To go long, you must let go of the need for speed.
You must trade the addiction to immediate movement
for the slow, steady discipline of meaningful progress.

You must learn to be still when others are panicking.
You must learn to move deliberately when others are rushing
blindly.
You must learn to value patience not as a weakness,
but as a rare and strategic strength.

The life built on speed is brittle.
It is vulnerable to collapse when the inevitable slow seasons
come.
It is addicted to momentum,
unable to sustain itself when the applause quiets and the pace
slows.

But the life built on patience is resilient.
It is rooted deeply enough to endure drought and storm alike.
It is strong enough to move slowly —
because it is moving toward something real.

Letting go of speed is not letting go of ambition.
It is letting go of the false urgency that dilutes ambition
into a frantic scramble.

It is choosing depth over haste,
substance over appearance,
endurance over acceleration.

It is trusting that what you are building
matters enough to take the time to build it well.

Because speed fades.
But what is built slowly, carefully, patiently —
it endures.

---

## Sacrificing the Ego's Need for Immediate Recognition

The ego is impatient.
It is always hungry,
always waiting for acknowledgment,
always craving the next moment of validation.

It feeds on recognition —
on being seen, being praised, being admired.

And it demands immediacy.
It does not want to wait for its rewards.
It does not want to endure the slow, silent years of unseen labor.
It wants to be known now.

It wants to be celebrated now.
It wants to be proven right now.

But the pursuit of immediate recognition is a trap.
It shifts your focus from the work to the audience.
It tempts you to measure your progress by applause
instead of by alignment with your deeper values.
It lures you into shaping your life for public consumption
rather than private excellence.

The ego's hunger for recognition is not easily satisfied.
It demands more and more —
more attention,
more praise,
more proof that you are succeeding by visible standards.

But what the ego does not understand
is that real success —
the kind that endures —
often grows in the dark,
away from the spotlight,
beyond the reach of quick approval.

To go long, you must sacrifice this need.
You must learn to labor without the audience.
You must learn to grow without the validation.
You must learn to become without the applause.

This sacrifice is not easy.
It is painful to watch others be celebrated
while your own work remains unseen.
It is difficult to resist the pull to make yourself more visible,
to win the approval that feels so close, so achievable.

But in giving up the need for immediate recognition,
you gain something deeper:
the freedom to build for the sake of the building,
the permission to grow slowly,
the strength to stay loyal to your path even when no one else
notices.

You gain the quiet confidence that comes from knowing
you are not working to be seen —
you are working to become.
You are not building for quick rewards —
you are building for lasting meaning.

The life built on the hunger for recognition is fragile.
It is forever chasing the next compliment,
forever vulnerable to the absence of applause.
It is externally controlled,
at the mercy of others' opinions,
others' attention spans.

But the life built on internal loyalty —
on the quiet, patient pursuit of mastery,
of integrity,
of substance —
is resilient.

It is the life that can withstand the long, invisible seasons.
It is the life that can outlast the noise of trends and fashions.
It is the life that endures when others fade.

To go long,
you must let the ego starve.
You must let the hunger for quick recognition die.
You must feed instead the deeper hunger —

for excellence,
for truth,
for becoming the kind of person
whose work speaks louder than any praise ever could.

---

# Chapter 15
# Patience as the Ultimate Edge

---

## Why Patience Outlasts Talent and Speed

---

Talent is dazzling.
It captures attention.
It announces itself early and loudly.
It seduces the world into believing that success is a matter of natural gift —
that some are born to rise quickly and stay aloft effortlessly.

Speed is thrilling.
It promises momentum.
It creates the illusion of inevitability —
as if moving fast is the same as moving well,
as if early gains guarantee lasting victories.

But time has a different scale of judgment.

Time reveals what talent cannot protect.
Time tests what speed cannot sustain.
Time sifts what shines quickly from what endures quietly.

In the long game, patience outlasts talent and speed.
Because talent is vulnerable to complacency.
And speed is vulnerable to burnout.
But patience —
patience is resilient.

Patience moves differently.
It does not demand immediate results.
It does not panic when progress slows.
It does not abandon the process when the rewards are delayed.

Patience trusts the deeper arc of growth.
It understands that mastery is not a product of natural ability
alone,
but of consistent effort compounded over years.

It understands that real progress often looks like no progress at all
—
that the most important growth happens invisibly,
beneath the surface,
in the slow, stubborn accumulation of skill and resilience.

Patience is not passive.
It is not sitting idly, hoping that things will eventually work out.
It is active.
It is engaged.
It is the discipline of steady, deliberate effort
without the need for constant reassurance.

It is the willingness to be overlooked now
to be undeniable later.
The willingness to be underestimated today
to be unshakable tomorrow.

Patience allows you to withstand the seasons of drought,
to keep moving when others have given up,
to build when others are chasing shortcuts.

It grants you an edge that the impatient will never have —
the edge of cumulative advantage.
The quiet, compounding gains that come only to those who stay
loyal to the work
long after the excitement has worn off.

Talent fades if it is not tended.
Speed falters if it is not grounded.
But patience —
patience endures.

In a world obsessed with fast outcomes and quick wins,
patience is a rare and powerful form of rebellion.
It is the quiet edge that does not glitter,
but cuts deeper and lasts longer.

Those who master patience do not just survive the long game.
They define it.
They outlast the talented who gave up,
the fast who burned out,
the restless who got lost.

Because in the end, the long game does not reward the most
gifted.
It rewards the most patient.

# The Invisible Compounding of Patient Effort

Most growth happens out of sight.
It happens in places no one is watching,
in moments no one is celebrating.

It happens slowly —
so slowly that even you, living inside it,
can barely feel the movement.

There are no instant victories in real progress.
There are no dramatic turning points where everything changes
overnight.
There are only small, repeated efforts —
the quiet discipline of showing up,
the quiet discipline of staying focused,
the quiet discipline of doing the work even when the results are
not visible.

Patient effort compounds.
Not in bursts,
but in layers.
Not in flashes,
but in foundations.

Every day you show up,
every day you practice,
every day you resist the urge to quit or pivot or chase something
easier —

you are laying down another layer of strength,
another layer of resilience,
another layer of mastery.

And though it looks like nothing is happening,
though it feels as if you are trapped in the same place,
something is shifting beneath the surface.

Skills are being refined.
Character is being forged.
Trust in your own process is being built.

This compounding is invisible for a long time.
The world will not reward it early.
You will not always recognize it yourself.
It will feel like too little, too late —
until it isn't.

Until one day,
what was slow becomes sudden.
What was invisible becomes undeniable.
What was incremental becomes exponential.

But by then, it will no longer feel like magic.
It will feel like the natural consequence of patient, persistent work
—

the quiet reward of those who stayed when others left,
who built when others doubted,
who endured when others demanded shortcuts.

The invisible compounding of patient effort is the true engine of
long-term success.
It is what separates the fleeting from the lasting,
the promising from the proven,
the dreamers from the builders.

It is why the long game cannot be hacked or hurried.
It is why those who endure patiently
eventually appear —
to the outside world —
as unstoppable forces.

But they know the truth:
It was not sudden.
It was not easy.
It was not luck.

It was the slow, silent compounding of effort
when no one was watching,
when no one was clapping,
when no one even knew they were still working.

Patience is not a virtue of the weak.
It is the strength of the builders.
The quiet power that, over time,
becomes unbreakable.

---

## Patience as a Competitive Advantage in a Reactive World

---

The world rewards reactivity.
It prizes speed, immediacy, visible response.
It celebrates those who jump first,

who move quickly,
who are always ready to react to the newest noise.

But the cost of reactivity is high —
fragmented attention,
scattered effort,
burned-out ambition.

In a reactive world, patience becomes an extraordinary advantage.

Patience is not inertia.
It is not slowness for its own sake.
It is deliberate resistance to the chaos of urgency.
It is a disciplined refusal to let the world's noise dictate your pace.

Patience allows you to see what others miss.
While the reactive rush into the obvious,
the patient wait for the unseen.
While the reactive chase what is immediate,
the patient invest in what is enduring.

Patience gives you time to think.
It gives you the space to plan,
to anticipate,
to move not first,
but best.

In business, in relationships, in creativity —
those who can pause,
those who can wait,
those who can act on principle instead of impulse —
build the structures that endure when the trends fade.

Patience grants clarity.
When others are blinded by urgency,
patience sharpens your focus.

It helps you distinguish between signal and noise,
between real opportunities and distractions dressed as
opportunities.

In a world addicted to instant validation,
patience frees you from the tyranny of public opinion.
It allows you to work without applause,
to build without the need for immediate affirmation,
to stay loyal to the long arc of your vision
when others have long since abandoned theirs.

Patience is not about doing nothing.
It is about doing the right thing
at the right time
in the right way —
even if that time is not now.

The patient builder knows that not every season is for harvesting.
Some seasons are for planting,
for cultivating,
for preparing quietly while the world rushes noisily toward quick
returns.

The patient strategist knows that not every move must be made
immediately.
Some moves must be prepared carefully,
executed precisely,
timed perfectly.

Patience is the discipline to wait without despair.
The courage to endure without recognition.
The strength to remain faithful when faster paths beckon with
easier rewards.

In a reactive world, patience is not just a virtue.
It is a competitive edge —
quiet, invisible, underestimated —
until it becomes undeniable.

Because when the reactive have burned themselves out,
when the quick have exhausted their strength chasing the next
thing and the next,
it is the patient who remain.

It is the patient who endure.
It is the patient who win.

---

## Living at the Pace of Endurance, Not Approval

---

Approval is fast.
It is immediate, reactive, volatile.
It rises and falls with trends, with moods, with moments.
One day you are praised; the next, forgotten.
One moment you are celebrated; the next, replaced.

Approval demands that you move at its speed —
that you chase it, adapt to it, obey it.
It demands that you prioritize visibility over depth,
popularity over principle,
momentary applause over meaningful progress.

But endurance moves differently.

Endurance ignores the pulse of public opinion.
It is not shaped by the noise of the moment.
It is not weakened by the absence of recognition.
It is not hurried by the shifting winds of approval.

Endurance moves according to a deeper rhythm —
a rhythm set not by what others expect,
but by what the work requires.

It is the rhythm of slow accumulation,
of deliberate progress,
of invisible foundations being laid,
quietly, persistently, far from the spotlight.

To live at the pace of endurance is to accept that you will often
move slower than the world demands.
You will often appear behind, overlooked, underestimated.
You will often be working when others are celebrating.
You will often be preparing when others are performing.

But this is the pace that builds what lasts.
It is the pace that constructs strength beneath the surface,
that refines skills others barely notice,
that shapes character in seasons of silence.

Living at the pace of endurance means choosing the slow work of
mastery
over the quick gratification of approval.
It means choosing to stay faithful to your path
even when the crowd is elsewhere,
even when the lights have moved on,
even when the rewards are still distant and unseen.

It means learning to take pride not in being seen,
but in staying true.

Not in being first,
but in being steadfast.

Approval will tempt you to abandon endurance.
It will whisper that you are falling behind,
that you must move faster,
that you must do more, be more, show more.

But endurance reminds you:
The goal is not to be admired.
The goal is to endure.
To build something that lasts beyond the trend cycle,
beyond the applause,
beyond the moment.

Endurance teaches you that what matters most
is not how quickly you rise,
but how deeply you are rooted.
Not how brightly you shine for a moment,
but how steadily you burn over time.

Living at the pace of endurance frees you from the tyranny of
approval.
It liberates you from the frantic chase of validation.
It anchors you to something slower, deeper, stronger.

Because in the end, the applause fades.
The trends shift.
The world moves on.

But endurance remains.
And the life built at its pace —
the slow, patient life of loyalty to what matters most —
outlasts them all.

# Epilogue
# Return to the Man at Gate B12

There are moments in life that do not reveal their meaning right
away.
Moments that pass quietly,
without ceremony,
without warning.

You live them, and they pass,
and you move on —
until something in you changes,
and you realize the moment has not left you after all.

It has been waiting.
It has been growing roots.

For years after that afternoon at Gate B12,
I thought little of the encounter.
A strange question from a stranger in an airport —
"How do you chop a tree 1000 kilometers away?"

It was easy to forget.
Easier still to dismiss.

But life has a way of circling back to the lessons you refused to
learn the first time.
It waits until you are ready,

215

until you have been broken open enough to see what was invisible before.

The years that followed were not gentle.
They stripped away the life I thought I had built.
They dismantled my ideas of success,
of certainty,
of control.

They tore through my plans,
through my identity,
through the fragile structures I had mistaken for foundations.

And when the dust settled,
when the noise quieted,
when the old ambitions lay in ruins,
the question returned.

How do you chop a tree 1000 kilometers away?

You begin long before anyone sees you move.
You sharpen the axe long before you swing it.
You study the wind, the grain, the ground.
You understand that the swing is only the last step —
the visible part of a process that is mostly invisible.

You understand that real change, real success, real mastery
is not a matter of force or speed or brilliance.
It is a matter of patience.
Of preparation.
Of silent, stubborn endurance.

It is a matter of learning to live above the noise,
beyond the hunger for quick victories and immediate applause.

It is a matter of seeing what others miss,
thinking in moves while others react to moments,
committing to the long game when others chase the short.

It is a matter of chopping the tree not with a single swing,
but with a thousand unseen decisions —
decisions to prepare,
to persist,
to endure.

The man at Gate B12 —
I never learned his name.
I never saw him again.

But his question stayed.
It became a riddle,
then a guidepost,
then a lighthouse.

And in the quiet that followed the collapse of everything I thought
I wanted,
it became a new way of living.

A way of seeing.
A way of thinking.
A way of moving —
slowly, patiently, deliberately —
in a world addicted to speed.

Not to arrive quickly.
Not to impress loudly.
But to build something that would last.

Something that could not be rushed.
Something that would not collapse under its own weight.
Something real.

How do you chop a tree 1000 kilometers away?

You begin before you're ready.
You move before you're seen.
You trust what is invisible.
You stay when it is hard to stay.
You endure when it is easier to abandon.

And one day, long after the noise has faded,
long after the crowds have moved on,
you hear a crack —
the sound of something giving way that no one else believed
would ever fall.

Not because you were the strongest.
Not because you were the fastest.

But because you were patient enough to finish what you started.

Because you understood what most forget:

Real mastery is invisible.
Until it isn't.

# Afterword

The long game is not about speed.
It is about endurance.

It is about seeing when others are blind,
thinking when others react,
staying when others run.

This is not a finish line.

It is a gate —
only one of many.

Walk slowly.
Walk wisely.
Walk on.

To the teachers who taught without knowing,
and to the lessons I resisted until I was ready to see.

# About the Author

**Ethan Starke** is a strategist, creator, and thinker whose work bridges endurance, leadership, and the art of living with intention.

He is the author of *Curate a Date* and *The Science of Letting Go*, and is devoted to helping people build meaningful lives in a noisy world.

*Fluency is born from stillness.*

www.ingramcontent.com/pod-product-compliance
Lightning Source LLC
Chambersburg PA
CBHW021623120626
46545CB00001B/363